Management
Challenges
for the
21st Century

Books by Peter F. Drucker

MANAGEMENT

Management Challenges for the 21st Century
Peter Drucker on the Profession of Management
Managing in a Time of Great Change
Managing for the Future
Managing the Non-Profit Organization
The Frontiers of Management
Innovation and Entrepreneurship
The Changing World of the Executive
Managing in Turbulent Times
Management: Tasks, Responsibilities, Practices
Technology, Management and Society
The Effective Executive
Managing for Results
The Practice of Management
Concept of the Corporation

ECONOMICS, POLITICS, SOCIETY

Post-Capitalist Society
Drucker on Asia
The Ecological Vision
The New Realities
Toward the Next Economics
The Pension Fund Revolution
Men, Ideas and Politics
The Age of Discontinuity
Landmarks of Tomorrow
America's Next Twenty Years
The New Society
The Future of Industrial Man
The End of Economic Man

AUTOBIOGRAPHY

Adventures of a Bystander

FICTION

The Temptation to Do Good
The Last of All Possible Worlds

Management Challenges for the 21st Century

PETER F. DRUCKER

HarperBusiness
An Imprint of HarperCollins*Publishers*

HarperCollins books may be purchased for educational, business, or sales promotional use. For information, please write to: Special Markets Department, HarperCollins Publishers Inc., 10 East 53rd Street, New York, New York 10022.

First HarperBusiness paperback edition published 2001.

Designed by Nancy Singer Olaguera

The Library of Congress has catalogued the hardcover edition as follows:
Drucker, Peter Ferdinand, 1909–
    Management challenges for the 21st century / Peter F. Drucker.
— 1st ed.
        p.   cm.
    ISBN 0-88730-998-4
    Includes index.
    1. Management — Forecasting. 2. Twenty-first century —
Forecasts. I. Title
HD30.27.D78 1999
658—dc21   99-17087

ISBN 0-88-730999-2 (pbk.)

06   ❖/RRD 20 19 18 17 16

Contents

Introduction: Tomorrow's "Hot" Issues

Where, readers may ask, is the discussion of COMPETITIVE STRATEGY, of LEADERSHIP, of CREATIVITY, of TEAMWORK, of TECHNOLOGY in a book on MANAGEMENT CHALLENGES? Where are the "HOT" ISSUES OF TODAY? But this is *the very reason* why they are *not* in this book. It deals exclusively with TOMORROW'S "Hot" Issues—the crucial, central, life-and-death issues that are *certain* to be the major challenges of tomorrow.

CERTAIN? Yes. For this is not a book of PREDICTIONS, not a book about the FUTURE. The challenges and issues discussed in it are already with us in every one of the developed countries and in most of the emerging ones (e.g., Korea or Turkey). They can already be identified, discussed, analyzed and prescribed for. Some people, someplace, are already working on them. But so far very few organizations do, and very few executives. Those who do work on these challenges today, and thus prepare themselves and their institutions for the new challenges, will be the leaders and dominate tomorrow. Those who wait until these challenges have indeed become "hot" issues are likely to fall behind, perhaps never to recover.

This book is thus a *Call for Action*.

These challenges are not arising out of today. THEY ARE DIFFERENT. In most cases they are at odds and incompatible with what is accepted and successful today. We live in a period of PROFOUND TRANSITION—and the changes are more radical perhaps than even those that ushered in the "Second Industrial

Revolution" of the middle of the 19th century, or the structural changes triggered by the Great Depression and the Second World War. READING this book will upset and disturb a good many people, as WRITING it disturbed me. For in many cases—for example, in the challenges inherent in the DISAPPEARING BIRTHRATE in the developed countries, or in the challenges to the individual, and to the employing organization, discussed in the final chapter on MANAGING ONESELF—the new realities and their demands require a REVERSAL of policies that have worked well for the last century and, even more, a change in the MINDSET of organizations as well as of individuals.

This is a MANAGEMENT BOOK. It intentionally leaves out BUSINESS CHALLENGES—even very important ones such as the question of whether the EURO will displace the U.S. dollar as the world's key currency, or what will SUCCEED the 19th century's most successful economic inventions, the commercial bank and the investment bank. It intentionally does not concern itself with ECONOMICS—even though the basic MANAGEMENT changes (e.g., the emergence of knowledge as the economy's key resource) will certainly necessitate radically new economic theory and equally radically new economic policy. The book does not concern itself with politics—not even with such crucial questions as whether Russia can and will recover as a political, military and economic power. It sticks with MANAGEMENT ISSUES.

There are good reasons for this. The issues this book discusses, the new social, demographic and economic REALITIES, are not issues that GOVERNMENT can successfully deal with. They are issues that will have profound impact on politics; but they are not political issues. They are not issues the Free Market can deal with. They are also not issues of ECONOMIC THEORY or even of ECONOMIC POLICY. They are issues that only MANAGEMENT and the INDIVIDUAL knowledge worker, professional or executive can tackle and resolve. They are surely going to be *debated* in the domestic politics of every developed and every emerging country. But their resolution will have to take place within the individual organization and will have to be worked out by the individual organization's MANAGEMENT—and by every single individual knowledge worker (and especially by every single executive) within the organization.

A great many of these organizations will, of course, be businesses. And a great many of the individual knowledge workers affected by these challenges will be employees of business or working with business. Yet this is a MANAGEMENT book rather than a BUSINESS management book. The challenges it presents affect ALL organizations of today's society. In fact, some of them will affect nonbusinesses even more, if only because a good many nonbusiness organizations—the university, for instance, or the hospital, let alone the government agency—are more rigid and less flexible than businesses are, and far more deeply rooted in the concepts, the assumptions, the policies of yesterday or even, as are universities, in the assumptions of the day before yesterday (i.e., of the 19th century).

How to use the book? I suggest you read a chapter at a time—they are long chapters. And then first ask: "What do these issues, these challenges MEAN for our organization and for me as a knowledge worker, a professional, an executive?" Once you have thought this through, ask: "What ACTION should our organization and I, the individual knowledge worker and/or executive, take to make the challenges of this chapter into OPPORTUNITIES for our organization and me?"

AND THEN GO TO WORK!

Peter F. Drucker
Claremont, California
New Year's Day 1999

1

Management's
New Paradigms

Why Assumptions Matter · Management Is *Business* Management · The *One Right* Organization · The *One Right* Way to Manage People · Technologies and End-Users Are Fixed and Given · Management's Scope Is *Legally* Defined · Management's Scope Is *Politically* Defined · The *Inside* Is Management's Domain

Introduction
Why Assumptions Matter

BASIC ASSUMPTIONS ABOUT REALITY are the PARADIGMS of a social science, such as management. They are usually held subconsciously by the scholars, the writers, the teachers, the practitioners in the field. Yet those assumptions largely determine what the discipline—scholars, writers, teachers, practitioners—assumes to be REALITY.

The discipline's basic assumptions about reality determine what it focuses on. They determine what a discipline considers "facts," and indeed what it considers the discipline itself to be all about. The assumptions also largely determine what is being disregarded in a discipline or is being pushed aside as an "annoying exception." They decide both what in a given discipline is being paid attention to and what is neglected or ignored.

A good example is what happened to the most insightful of the earlier management scholars: Mary Parker Follett (1868-1933).* Because her assumptions did not fit the realities which the budding discipline of management assumed in the 1930s and 1940s, she became a "nonperson" even before her death in 1932, with her work practically forgotten for twenty-five years or more. And yet we now know that her basic assumptions regarding society, people and management were far closer to reality than those on which the management people then based themselves—and still largely base themselves today.

Yet, despite their importance, the assumptions are rarely analyzed, rarely studied, rarely challenged—indeed rarely even made explicit.

For a social discipline such as management the assumptions are actually a good deal more important than are the paradigms

---

*On this see my introduction to *Mary Parker Follett, Prophet of Management* (Boston: Harvard Business School Press, 1995).

for a natural science. The paradigm—that is, the prevailing general theory—has no impact on the natural universe. Whether the paradigm states that the sun rotates around the earth or that, on the contrary, the earth rotates around the sun has no effect on sun and earth. A natural science deals with the behavior of OBJECTS. But a social discipline such as management deals with the behavior of PEOPLE and HUMAN INSTITUTIONS. Practitioners will therefore tend to act and to behave as the discipline's assumptions tell them to. Even more important, the reality of a natural science, the physical universe and its laws, do not change (or if they do only over eons rather than over centuries, let alone over decades). The social universe has no "natural laws" of this kind. It is thus subject to continuous change. And this means that assumptions that were valid yesterday can become invalid and, indeed, totally misleading in no time at all.

Everyone these days preaches the team as the "right" organization for every task. (I myself began to preach teams as early as 1954 and especially in my 1973 book *Management: Tasks, Responsibilities, Practices*.) Underlying the present orthodoxy regarding teams is a basic assumption held practically by all management theorists and by most practitioners since the earliest days of thinking about organization, that is, since Henri Fayol in France and Walter Rathenau in Germany around 1900: There is—or, at least, there MUST be—ONE right organization. And what matters most is not whether the team is indeed "the answer" (so far there is not too much evidence for it), but, as will be discussed a little later, that the basic assumption of the one right organization is no longer tenable.

What matters most in a social discipline such as management are therefore the basic assumptions. And a CHANGE in the basic assumptions matters even more.

Since the study of management first began—and it truly did

not emerge until the 1930s—TWO SETS of assumptions regarding the REALITIES of management have been held by most scholars, most writers and most practitioners:

One set of assumptions underlies the DISCIPLINE of management:

1. Management is *Business* Management.

2. There is—or there must be—ONE right *organization structure*.

3. There is—or there must be—ONE right way to *manage people*.

Another set of assumptions underlies the PRACTICE of Management:

1. Technologies, markets and end-uses are *given*.

2. Management's scope is *legally* defined.

3. Management is internally focused.

4. The economy as defined by national boundaries is the "ecology" of enterprise and management.

For most of this period—at least until the early 1980s—all but the first of these assumptions were close enough to reality to be operational, whether for research, for writing, for teaching or for practicing management. By now all of them have outlived their usefulness. They are close to being caricatures. They are now so far removed from actual reality that they are becoming obstacles to the Theory and even more serious obstacles to the Practice of management. Indeed, reality is fast becoming the very opposite of what these assumptions claim it to be. It is high time therefore to think through these assumptions and to try to formulate the NEW ASSUMPTIONS that now have to inform both the study and the practice of management.

I
Management Is Business *Management*

For most people, inside and outside management, this assumption is taken as self-evident. Indeed management writers, management practitioners and the laity do not even hear the word "management"; they automatically hear BUSINESS MANAGEMENT.

This assumption regarding the universe of management is of fairly recent origin. Before the 1930s the few writers and thinkers who concerned themselves with management—beginning with Frederick Winslow Taylor around the turn of the century and ending with Chester Barnard just before World War II—all assumed that business management is just a subspecies of general management and basically no more different from the management of any other organization than one breed of dogs is from another breed of dogs.

The first *practical* application of management theory did not take place in a business but in nonprofits and government agencies. Frederick Winslow Taylor (1856–1915), the inventor of "Scientific Management," in all probability also coined the terms "Management" and "Consultant" in their present meaning. On his calling card he identified himself as "Consultant to Management"—and he explained that he had intentionally chosen these new and strange terms to shock potential clients into awareness of his offering something totally new. But Taylor did not cite a business but the nonprofit Mayo Clinic as the "perfect example" of "Scientific Management" in his 1912 testimony before the Congress which first made the United States management-conscious. And the most publicized application of Taylor's "Scientific Management" (though aborted by union pressure) was not in a business but in the government-owned and government-run Watertown Arsenal of the U.S. Army.

The first job to which the term "Manager" in its present meaning was applied was not in business. It was the City Manager—an American invention of the early years of the century. The first conscious and systematic application of "management principles" similarly was not in a business. It was the reorganization of the U.S. Army in 1901 by Elihu Root (1845-1937), Theodore Roosevelt's Secretary of War.

The first Management Congress—Prague in 1922— was not organized by business people but by Herbert Hoover, then U.S. Secretary of Commerce, and Thomas Masaryk, a world-famous historian and the founding President of the new Czechoslovak Republic. And Mary Parker Follett, whose work on Management began at roughly the same time, never differentiated between business management and nonbusiness management. She talked of the management of organizations, to all of which the same principles applied.

What led to the identification of Management with Business Management was the Great Depression with its hostility to business and its contempt for business executives. In order not to be tarred with the business brush, management in the public sector was rechristened "Public Administration" and proclaimed a separate discipline—with its own university departments, its own terminology, its own career ladder. At the same time—and for the same reason—what had begun as a study of management in the rapidly growing hospital (e.g., by Raymond Sloan, the younger brother of GM's Alfred Sloan) was split off as a separate discipline and christened "Hospital Administration."

Not to be called "management" was, in other words, "political correctness" in the Depression years.

In the postwar period, however, the fashion turned. By 1950 BUSINESS had become a "good word"—largely the result of the performance during World War II of American *business* management. And then very soon "business management" became "politically correct" as a field of study, above all. And ever since, management has remained identified in the public mind as well as in academia with "business management."

Now, however, we are beginning to unmake this sixty-year-old mistake—as witness the renaming of so many "business schools" into "schools of management," the rapidly growing offerings in "nonprofit management" by these schools, the emergence of "executive management programs" recruiting both business and nonbusiness executives or the emergence of Departments of "Pastoral Management" in divinity schools.

But the assumption that Management is Business Management still persists. It is therefore important to assert—and to do so loudly—that Management is NOT Business Management—any more than, say, Medicine is Obstetrics.

There are, of course, differences in management between different organizations—Mission defines Strategy, after all, and Strategy defines Structure. There surely are differences between managing a chain of retail stores and managing a Catholic diocese (though amazingly fewer than either chain stores or bishops believe); between managing an air base, a hospital and a software company. But the greatest differences are in the terms individual organizations use. Otherwise the differences are mainly in application rather than in principles. There are not even tremendous differences in tasks and challenges. The executives of all these organizations spend, for instance, about the same amount of their time on people problems—and the people problems are almost always the same. Ninety percent or so of what each of these organizations is concerned with is generic. And the differences in respect to the last 10 percent are no greater between businesses and nonbusinesses than they are between businesses in different industries, for example, between a multinational bank and a toy manufacturer. In every organization—business or nonbusiness alike—only the last 10 percent of management has to be fitted to the organization's specific mission, its specific culture, its specific history and its specific vocabulary.

That Management is not Business Management is particularly important as the growth sector of a *developed society* in the 21st century is most unlikely to be business—in fact, business has not even been the growth sector of the 20th century in developed societies. A far smaller proportion of the working population in every developed country is now engaged in economic activity, that is, in "business," than it was a hundred years ago. Then virtually everybody in the working population made his or her living in economic activities (e.g., farming). The growth sectors in the 20th century in developed countries have been in "nonbusiness"—in government, in the professions, in health care, in education. As an employer and a source of livelihood business has been shrinking steadily for a hundred years (or at least since World War I). And insofar as we can predict, the growth sector in the 21st century in developed countries will not be "business," that is, organized *economic* activity. It is likely to be the nonprofit social sector. And that is also the sector where management is today most needed and where systematic, principled, theory-based management can yield the greatest results the fastest.

The first Conclusion of this analysis of the ASSUMPTIONS that must underlie Management to make productive both its study and its practice is therefore:

Management is the specific and distinguishing organ of any and all organizations.

II
The One Right *Organization*

Concern with management and its study began with the sudden emergence of large organizations—business, governmental civil service, the large standing army—which was the novelty of late-19th-century society.

And from the very beginning more than a century ago, the study of organization has rested on one assumption:

There is—or there must be—one right organization.

What is presented as the "one right organization" has changed more than once. But the search for the one right organization has continued and continues today.

Organization structure in business was first tackled in France around the turn of the century, by Henri Fayol (1841–1925), the head of one of Europe's largest but also totally disorganized enterprises, a coal-mining company. (He did not, however, publish his book until 1916.) Practitioners were also the first ones concerned with organization in the United States and at about the same time: John J. Rockefeller, Sr.; J. P. Morgan, and especially Andrew Carnegie (who still deserves to be studied and who had the most lasting impact). A little later Elihu Root applied organization theory to the U.S. Army, as already mentioned—and it is hardly coincidence that Root had been Carnegie's legal adviser. At the same time, Georg Siemens (1839–1901), the founder in 1870 of the Deutsche Bank, used (around 1895) the organization concepts of his friend Fayol to save the rapidly floundering Siemens Electric Company that his cousin Werner Siemens (1816–1892) had founded but had left leaderless at his death.

Yet the need for organization structure was by no means obvious to everybody in these early years.

Frederick Winslow Taylor did not see it at all. Until his death he wrote and talked of "the owners and their helpers." And it was on this concept, that is, on a non-structure, that Henry Ford (1863–1947), up to the time of his death, tried to run what for many years (until the late 1920s) was the world's largest manufacturing company.

It was World War I that made clear the need for a formal organization structure. But it was also World War I that showed that Fayol's (and Carnegie's) functional structure was not the one right organization. Immediately after World War I first Pierre S. Du Pont (1870–1954) and then Alfred Sloan (1875–1966) developed Decentralization. And now, in the last few years, we have come to tout the "Team" as the one right organization for pretty much everything.

By now, however, it should have become clear that there is no such thing as the one right organization. There are only organizations, each of which has distinct strengths, distinct limitations and specific applications. It has become clear that organization is not an absolute. It is a *tool* for making people productive in working together. As such, a given organization structure fits certain tasks in certain conditions and at certain times.

One hears a great deal today about "the end of hierarchy." This is blatant nonsense. In any institution there has to be a final authority, that is, a "boss"—someone who can make the final decisions and who can expect them to be obeyed. In a situation of common peril—and every institution is likely to encounter it sooner or later—survival of all depends on clear command. If the ship goes down, the captain does not call a meeting, the captain gives an order. And if the ship is to be saved, everyone must obey the order, must know exactly where to go and what to do, and do it without "participation" or argument. "Hierarchy," and the unquestioning acceptance of it by everyone in the organization, is the only hope in a crisis.

Other situations within the same institution require deliberation. Others still require teamwork—and so on.

Organization Theory assumes that institutions are homogeneous and that, therefore, the entire enterprise should be organized the same way.

Fayol assumed a "typical manufacturing enterprise." Alfred Sloan in the 1920s organized each of General Motors' decentralized divisions exactly the same way. Thirty years later, in the massive reorganization of the (American) General Electric Company in the early 1950s, it was still considered "heresy" to organize a small unit of a few dozen researchers engaged solely on development work for the U.S. Air Force differently from huge "departments" employing several thousand people and manufacturing a standard product, for example, a toaster for the kitchen. The small development group was actually saddled with a manufacturing manager, a personnel manager, a financial manager, and a public relations manager.

But in any one enterprise—probably even in Fayol's "typical manufacturing company"—there is need for a number of different organization structures coexisting side by side.

Managing foreign currency exposure is an increasingly critical—and increasingly difficult—task in a world economy. It requires total centralization. No one unit of the enterprise can be permitted to handle its own foreign currency exposures. But in the same enterprise servicing the customer, especially in high-tech areas, requires almost complete local autonomy—going way beyond traditional decentralization. Each of the individual service people has to be the "boss," with the rest of the organization taking its direction from them.

Certain forms of research require a strict functional organization with all specialists "playing their instrument" by themselves. Other kinds of research, however, especially research that involves decision making at an early stage (e.g., some pharmaceutical research), require teamwork from the beginning. And the two kinds of research often occur side by side and in the same research organization.

The belief that there must be one right organization is closely tied to the fallacy that Management is Business Management. If earlier students of management had not been blinkered by this fallacy but had looked at nonbusinesses, they would soon have found that there are vast differences in organization structure according to the nature of the task.

A Catholic diocese is organized very differently from an opera. A modern army is organized very differently from a hospital. But also, typically, these institutions have more than one organization structure. In the Catholic diocese, for instance, the bishop is the absolute authority in certain areas, a constitutional monarch in others (severely limited, for instance, in his right to discipline his diocesan clergy) and virtually powerless in others—he cannot, for instance, visit a parish in his diocese unless the parish priest invites him to do so. The bishop appoints the members of the diocesan court—though custom indicates which of his clerics are eligible for such an appointment. But once that court is appointed it, rather than the bishop, has exclusive jurisdiction in a great many areas.

There are indeed some "principles" of organization.

One is surely that organization has to be transparent. People have to know and have to understand the organization structure they are supposed to work in. This sounds obvious—but it is far too often violated in most institutions (even in the military).

Another principle I have already mentioned: Someone in the organization must have the authority to make the final decision in a given area. And someone must clearly be in command in a CRISIS. It also is a sound principle that authority be commensurate with responsibility.

It is a sound principle that one person in an organization should have only one "master." There is wisdom to the old proverb of the Roman Law that a slave who has three masters is a free man. It is a very old principle of human relations that no one should be put into a conflict of loyalties—and having more than one "master" creates such a conflict (which, by the way, is the reason that the "Jazz Combo" team, so popular now, is so difficult—every one of its members has two masters, the head of the specialty function, for example, engineering, and the team leader). It is a sound, structural principle to have the fewest layers, that is, to have an organization that is as "flat" as possible—if only because, as Information Theory tells us, "every relay doubles the noise and cuts the message in half."

But these principles do not tell us *what to do*. They only tell us what not to do. They do not tell us what will work. They tell us what is unlikely to work. These principles are not too different from the ones that inform an architect's work. They do not tell him what kind of building to build. They tell him what the restraints are. And this is pretty much what the various principles of organization structure do.

One implication: *Individuals* will have to be able to work at one and the same time in different organization structures. For one task they will work in a team. But for another task they will have to work—and at the same time—in a command and control structure. The same individual who is a "boss" within his or her own organization is a "partner" in an alliance, a minority participation, a joint venture and so on. Organizations, in other words, will have to become part of the executive's toolbox.

Even more important: We need to go to work on studying the strengths and the limitations of different organizations. For what tasks are what organizations most suitable? For what tasks are what organizations least suitable? And when, in the performance of a task, should we switch from one kind of organization to another?

This analysis is perhaps most needed for the currently "politically correct" organization: the team.

It is generally assumed today that there is only one kind of team—call it the Jazz Combo—and that it fits every task. Actually there are at least half a dozen—perhaps a full dozen—very different teams, each with its own area of application, each with its own limitations and difficulties, and each requiring different management. The team that is popular now, the Jazz Combo, is arguably the most difficult one, the one most difficult to make work and the one with the most severe limitations. Unless we work out, and fast, what a given team is suited for, and what a given team is not suited for, teams will become discredited as "just another fad" within a few short years. Yet teams are important. Where they do belong and where they do work, they are the most effective organization.

And surely we will have to study and to use "mixed" structures rather than only the "pure," "one right organization," which organization theory—and largely also organization practice—still believes in.

One example: the dozen or more highly trained people needed to perform open-heart surgery such as a heart bypass operation. They can be seen as a pure—indeed an extreme—example of Fayol's "functional organization," with each member—the lead surgeon, the two assistant surgeons, the anesthesiologist, the two nurses who prepare the patient for the operation, the three nurses who assist at the operation, the two or three nurses and the resident in the recovery room and intensive care unit, the respiratory technician running the heart-lung machine, the three or four electronic technicians—each doing ONE, and only one task and never, never doing anything else. Yet these people look upon themselves as a "team"—and are seen as a team by everyone in the hospital. They are indeed a "team" in that each member—immediately and without anyone's giving an order or saying one word—changes HOW he or she is doing the job with the slightest change in the rhythm, the progress, the flow of the operation.

One area in which research and study are particularly needed is the ORGANIZATION OF TOP MANAGEMENT.

Concern with organization actually began with the first conscious design of the top management job—the AMERICAN CONSTITUTION. This design did solve for the first time what had been the oldest organization problem of political society and one that no earlier political system could solve: the succession problem. The Constitution made sure that there would always be a chief executive officer fully legitimate, fully authorized and (hopefully) prepared for the job—and yet not threatening the authority of the present incumbent as did the crown princes of yore. In respect to the structure of top management in nonpolitical organizations, work also antedates formal organization theory. Georg Siemens—already mentioned as the founder of the Deutsche Bank and as the savior, through imposing formal organization structure, of his cousin's electric company (and both the Deutsche Bank and the Siemens Electric Company are still their country's largest businesses in their respective industries)—designed what to this day is the legal structure of top management in Germany (and, with slight variations, in Central and Northern Europe as well): a team of equal partners, each of whom, however, is a FUNCTIONAL expert and all but autonomous in his or her area, with the entire group then electing a "SPEAKER" who is not a "boss" but a "leader."

Yet I doubt that anyone would assert that we really know how to organize the top management job, whether in a business, a university, a hospital or even a modern church.

One clear sign is the growing disparity between our rhetoric and our practice: We talk incessantly about "teams"—and every study comes to the conclusion that the top management job does indeed require a team. Yet we now *practice*—and not only in American industry—the most extreme "personality cult" of CEO supermen. And no one seems to pay the slightest attention in our present worship of these larger-than-life CEOs to the question of how and by what process they are to be succeeded—and yet, succession has always been the ultimate test of any top management and the ultimate test of any institution.

There is, in other words, an enormous amount of work to be done in organizational theory and organization practice—even though both are the oldest areas of organized work and organized practice in management.

The pioneers of management a century ago were right. *Organizational Structure is needed.* The modern enterprise—whether business, civil service, university, hospital, large church or large military—needs organization just as any biological organization beyond the ameba needs structure. But the pioneers were wrong in their assumption that there is—or should be—one right organization. Just as there are a great number of different structures for biological organizations, so there are a number of organizations for the social organism that is the modern institution. Instead of searching for the right organization, management needs to learn to look for, to develop, to test

The organization that fits the task.

III
The **One Right** *Way to Manage People*

In no other area are the basic traditional assumptions held as firmly—though mostly subconsciously—as in respect to people and their management. And in no other area are they so totally at odds with reality and so totally counterproductive.

"*There is one right way to manage people—or at least there should be.*" This assumption underlies practically every book or paper on the management of people.

Its most quoted exposition is Douglas McGregor's book *The Human Side of Enterprise* (1960), which asserted that managements have to choose between two and only two different ways of managing people, "Theory X" and "Theory Y," and which then asserted that Theory Y is the only sound one. (A little earlier I had said pretty much the same thing in my 1954 book *The Practice of Management*.) A few years later Abraham H. Maslow (1908-1970) showed in his *Eupsychian Management* (1962; new edition 1995 entitled *Maslow on Management*) that both McGregor and I were dead wrong. He showed conclusively that different people have to be managed differently.

I became an immediate convert—Maslow's evidence is over-whelming. But to date very few people have paid much attention.

On this fundamental assumption that there is—or at least should be—one and only one right way to manage people, rest all the other assumptions about people in organizations and their management.

One of these assumptions is that the people who work for an

organization are *employees* of the organization, working full-time, and dependent on the organization for their livelihood and their careers. Another such assumption is that the people who work for an organization are *subordinates*. Indeed, it is assumed that the great majority of these people have either no skill or low skills and do what they are being assigned to do.

Eighty years ago, when these assumptions were first formulated, during and at the end of WWI, they conformed close enough to reality to be considered valid. Today every one of them has become untenable. The majority of people who work for an organization may still be employees of the organization. But a very large and steadily growing minority—though working *for* the organization—are no longer its employees, let alone its full-time employees. They work for an outsourcing contractor, for example, the outsourcing firm that provides maintenance in a hospital or a manufacturing plant, or the outsourcing firm that runs the data processing system for a government agency or a business. They are "temps" or part-timers. Increasingly they are individual contractors working on a retainer or for a specific contractual period; this is particularly true of the most knowledgeable and therefore the most valuable people working for the organization.

Even if employed full-time by the organization, fewer and fewer people are "subordinates"—even in fairly low-level jobs. Increasingly they are "knowledge workers." And knowledge workers are not subordinates; they are "associates." For, once beyond the apprentice stage, knowledge workers must know more about their job than their boss does—or else they are no good at all. In fact, that they know more about their job than anybody else in the organization is part of the definition of knowledge workers.

> The engineer servicing a customer does not know more about the product than the engineering manager does. But he knows more about the customer—and that may be more important than product knowledge. The meteorologist on an air base is vastly inferior in rank to the air base commander. But he is of no use unless he knows infinitely more about weather forecasting than the air base commander does. The mechanic servicing an airliner knows

far more about the technical condition of the plane than the airport manager of the airline to whom he reports, and so on.

Add to this that today's "superiors" usually have not held the jobs their "subordinates" hold—as they did only a few short decades ago and as still is widely assumed they do.

A regimental commander in the army, only a few decades ago, had held every one of the jobs of his subordinates—battalion commander, company commander, platoon commander. The only difference in these respective jobs between the lowly platoon commander and the lordly regimental commander was in the number of people each commands; the work they did was exactly alike. To be sure, today's regimental commanders have commanded troops earlier in their careers—but often for a short period only. They also have advanced through captain and major. But for most of their careers they have held very different assignments—in staff jobs, in research jobs, in teaching jobs, attached to an embassy abroad and so on. They simply can no longer assume that they know what their "subordinate," the captain in charge of a company, is doing or trying to do—they have been captains, of course, but they may have never commanded a company.

Similarly, the vice-president of marketing may have come up the sales route. He or she knows a great deal about selling. But he or she knows nothing about market research, pricing, packaging, service, sales forecasting. The marketing vice-president therefore cannot possibly tell the experts in the marketing department what they should be doing, and how. Yet they are supposed to be the marketing vice-president's "subordinates"—and the marketing vice-president is definitely responsible for their performance and for their contribution to the company's marketing efforts.

The same is true for the hospital administrator or the hospital's medical director in respect to the trained knowledge workers in the clinical laboratory or in physical therapy.

To be sure, these associates are "subordinates" in that they depend on the "boss" when it comes to being hired or fired, promoted, appraised and so on. But in his or her own job the superior can perform only if these so-called subordinates take responsibility for *educating* him or her, that is, for making the "superior" understand what market research or physical therapy can do and should be doing, and what "results" are in their respective areas. In turn, these "subordinates" depend on the superior for direction. They depend on the superior to tell them what the "score" is.

Their relationship, in other words, is far more like that between the conductor of an orchestra and the instrumentalist than it is like the traditional superior/subordinate relationship. The superior in an organization employing knowledge workers cannot, as a rule, do the work of the supposed subordinate any more than the conductor of an orchestra can play the tuba. In turn, the knowledge worker is dependent on the superior to give direction and, above all, to define what the "score" is for the entire organization, that is, what are standards and values, performance and results. And just as an orchestra can sabotage even the ablest conductor—and certainly even the most autocratic one—a knowledge organization can easily sabotage even the ablest, let alone the most autocratic, superior.

Altogether, an increasing number of people who are full-time employees have to be managed as if they were *volunteers*. They are paid, to be sure. But knowledge workers have mobility. They can leave. They own their "means of production," which is their knowledge. (See on this also Chapter Six.)

We have known for fifty years that money alone does not motivate to perform. Dissatisfaction with money grossly demotivates. Satisfaction with money is, however, mainly a "hygiene factor," as Frederick Herzberg called it all of forty years ago in his 1959 book *The Motivation to Work*. What motivates—and especially what motivates knowledge workers—is what motivates volunteers. Volunteers, we know, have to get *more* satisfaction from their work than paid employees, precisely because they do not get a paycheck. They need, above all, challenge. They need to know the organization's mission and to believe in it. They need continuous training. They need to see results.

Implicit in this is that different groups in the work population have to be managed differently, and that the same group in the work population has to be managed differently at different times. Increasingly "employees" have to be managed as "partners"—and it is the definition of a partnership that all partners are equal. It is also the definition of a partnership that partners cannot be ordered. They have to be persuaded. Increasingly, therefore, the management of people is a "marketing job." And in marketing one does not begin with the question: "What do *we* want?" One begins with the question: "What does the other party want? What are its values? What are its goals? What does it consider results?" And this is neither "Theory X" nor "Theory Y," nor any other specific theory of *managing* people.

Maybe we will have to redefine the task altogether. It may not be "managing the work of people." The starting point both in theory and in practice may have to be "managing for performance." The starting point may be a definition of results—just as the starting points of both the orchestra conductor and the football coach are the score.

The productivity of the knowledge worker is likely to become the center of the management of people, just as the work on the productivity of the manual worker became the center of managing people a hundred years ago, that is, since Frederick W. Taylor. This will require, above all, very different assumptions about people in organizations and their work:

One does not "manage" people.

The task is to lead people.

And the goal is to make productive the specific strengths and knowledge of each individual.

IV
Technologies and End-Users Are Fixed and Given

Four major assumptions, as said above, have been underlying the PRACTICE of Management all along—in fact for much longer than there has been a DISCIPLINE of Management.

The assumptions about technology and end-users to a very large extent underlie the rise of modern business and of the modern economy altogether. They go back to the very early days of the Industrial Revolution.

When the textile industry first developed out of what had been cottage industries it was assumed—and with complete validity—that the textile industry had its own unique technology. The same was true in respect to coal mining, and of any of the other industries that arose in the late 18th century and the first half of the 19th century. The first one to understand this and to base a major enterprise on it was also one of the first men to develop what we would today call a modern business, the German Werner Siemens (1816–1892). It led him in 1869 to hire the first university-trained scientist to start a modern research lab—devoted exclusively to what we would now call electronics, and based on a clear understanding that electronics (in those days called "low-voltage") was distinct and separate from all other industries, and had its distinct and separate technology.

Out of this insight grew not only Siemens's own company with its own research lab, but also the German chemical industry, which assumed worldwide leadership because it based itself on the assumption that chemistry—and especially organic chemistry—had its own unique technology. Out of it then grew all the other major leading companies the world over, whether the American electrical and chemical companies, the automobile companies, the telephone companies and so on. Out of this insight then grew what may well be the most successful invention of the 19th century, the research laboratory—the last one almost a century after Siemens's, the 1950 lab of IBM—and at around the same time the research labs of the major pharmaceutical companies as they emerged as a worldwide industry after World War II.

By now these assumptions have become untenable. The best example is of course the pharmaceutical industry, which increasingly has come to depend on technologies that are fundamentally different from the technologies on which the pharmaceutical research lab is based: genetics, for instance, microbiology, molecular biology, medical electronics and so on.

> But the same thing has happened in the automobile industry, which increasingly has become dependent on electronics, and on the computer. It has happened to the steel industry, which increasingly has become dependent on materials sciences of which the original steel companies were totally ignorant—and largely still are. It has happened to the paper industry—the list could be continued indefinitely.

In the 19th century and throughout the first half of the 20th century, it could be taken for granted that technologies outside one's own industry had no, or at least only minimal, impact on the industry. Now the assumption to start with is that the technologies that are likely to have the greatest impact on a company and an industry are technologies outside its own field.

The original assumption was of course that one's own research lab would and could produce everything the company—or the company's industry—needed. And in turn the assumption was that everything that this research lab produced would be used in and by the industry that it served.

This, for instance, was the clear foundation of what was probably the most successful of all the great research labs of the last hundred years, the Bell Labs of the American telephone system. Founded in the early 1920s, the Bell Labs until the late 1960s did indeed produce practically every new knowledge and every new technology the telephone industry needed. And in turn practically everything the Bell Labs scientists produced found its main use in the telephone system. This changed drastically with what was probably the Bell Labs's greatest scientific achievement: the transistor. The telephone company itself did become a heavy user of the transistor. But the main uses of the transistor were outside the telephone system. This was so unexpected that the Bell Telephone Company, when the transistor was first developed, virtually gave it away—it did not see enough use for it within the telephone system. But it also did not see any use for it outside it. And so what was the most revolutionary development that came out of the Bell Labs—and certainly the most valuable one—was sold freely to all comers for the paltry sum of $25,000. It is on this total failure of the Bell Labs to understand the significance of its own achievement that practically all modern electronic companies outside of the telephone are based.

Conversely, the things that have revolutionized the telephone system—such as digital switching or the fiberglass cable—did not come out of the Bell Labs. They came out of technologies that were foreign to telephone technology. And this has been typical altogether of the last thirty to fifty years—and it is increasingly becoming more typical of every industry.

Technologies, unlike the 19th-century technologies, no longer run in parallel. They constantly crisscross. Constantly, something in a technology of which people in a given industry have barely heard (just as the people in the pharmaceutical industry had never heard of genetics, let alone of medical electronics) revolutionizes an industry and its technology. Constantly, such outside technologies force an industry to learn, to acquire, to adapt, to change its very mindset, let alone its technical knowledge. The basic assumptions of genetics are alien to a pharmacologist—and yet genetics is rapidly revolutionizing the pharmaceutical industry. And the mindset of the geneticist is so different that so far, no major pharmaceutical company has been able to integrate genetics successfully into its own research program. It can only get access to genetics by alliances with outsiders, whether through minority participation in a genetics company or through an agreement with a university genetics department.

Equally important to the rise of 19th- and early-20th-century industry and companies was a second assumption: End-uses are fixed and given. For a certain end-use, for example, to put beer into containers, there may have been extreme competition between various suppliers of containers. But all of them, until recently, were glass companies, and there was only one way of putting beer into containers, a glass bottle.

Similarly, as soon as steel became available, that is, beginning in the last decades of the 19th century, rails for railroads were to be made from steel and from nothing else. As soon as electricity began to be transmitted over any distance, the wire had to be made from copper. And the same assumption applied to services. The credit needs of a business could only be supplied by a commercial loan from a commercial bank. The post office had a "natural monopoly" on transporting and delivering written and printed communications. There were two ways of getting fed: cooking for oneself at home or going out to a restaurant.

This was accepted as obvious not only by business, industry and the consumer, but by governments as well. The American regulation of business rests on the assumptions that to every industry pertains a unique technology and that to every end-use pertains a specific and unique product or service. These are the assumptions on which Anti-Trust was based. And to this day Anti-Trust concerns itself with the domination of the market in glass bottles and pays little attention to the fact that beer increasingly is not put into glass bottles but into cans (or, vice versa, Anti-Trust concerns itself exclusively with the concentration of supply in respect to metal containers for beer, paying no attention to the fact that beer is still being put into glass bottles, but also increasingly into plastic cans). As late as the mid-twenties the U.S. Supreme Court decided that there were two and only two mutually exclusive and non-competitive ways for telecommunication—the spoken word went via telephone and the written word went via telegraph. And ten years later during the Depression, the Congress of the United States separated investment banking from commercial banking, each to be set up in separate institutions and each having its own exclusive end-use.

But since WWII end-uses are not uniquely tied any more to a certain product or service. The plastics of course were the first major exception to the rule. But by now it is clear that it is not just one material moving in on what was considered the "turf" of another one. Increasingly the same want is being satisfied by very different means. It is the *want* that is unique, and not the means to satisfy it.

As late as the beginning of WWII, news was basically the monopoly of the newspaper—an 18th-century invention that saw its biggest growth in the early years of the 20th century. By now there are several competing ways to deliver news: still the printed newspaper, increasingly the same newspaper delivered on-line through the Internet, radio, television, separate news organizations that use only electronics—as is increasingly the case with economic and business news—and quite a few additional ones.

The U.S. Glass-Steagall Act of the Depression years not only attempted to prevent commercial banks from doing business in the investment market, it also tried to prevent investment bankers from doing commercial banking business and thus tried to give banks a monopoly on lending. One paradoxical result was that this act, intended to establish the monopoly position of the bank in the commercial market, has given the commercial market to the investment bankers. By a quirk of American law (a Supreme Court decision of the 1920s) "commercial paper" (the American equivalent to the European Bill of Exchange) was classified as a "security." This then enabled the investment bankers after 1960 to become the dominant force in the commercial banking business, that is, to replace increasingly the banks' commercial loan with the investment bankers' "commercial paper."

But increasingly in all developed countries the fastest-growing source of commercial credit is neither the commercial bank nor the investment bank. It is the credit card in its various forms. A still fairly small but rapidly growing number of credit card customers have multiple credit cards—some as many as twenty-five or thirty. They use these cards to obtain and to maintain a level of credit far beyond their creditworthiness. That the interest rate is very high does not seem to bother them, since they do not have any intention anyhow of paying off the loans. They manipulate them by shifting the outstanding balance from one card to the other so that they are never forced to pay more than very small, minimum amounts. The credit card has thus become what used to be called "legal tender." Nobody knows how big this new form of money has become—but it is clearly a new form of money. And it has already become so big as to make almost meaningless the figures for money in circulation, whether M1 or M2 or M3, on which central banks and economists base their theories and their forecasts.

And then there is the new "basic resource" information. It differs radically from all other commodities in that it does not stand under the scarcity theorem. On the contrary, it stands under an abundance theorem. If I sell a thing—for example, a book—I no longer have the book. If I impart information, I still have it. And in fact, information becomes more valuable the more people have it. What this means for economics is well beyond the scope of this book—though it is clear that it will force us radically to revise basic economic theory. But it also means a good deal for management. Increasingly basic assumptions will have to be changed. Information does not pertain to any industry or to any business. Information also does not have any one end-use, nor does any end-use require a particular kind of information or depend on one particular kind of information.

Management therefore now has to start out with the assumption that there is no one technology that pertains to any industry and that, on the contrary, all technologies are capable—and indeed likely—to be of major importance to any industry and to have impact on any industry. Management similarly has to start with the assumption that there is no one given end-use for any product or service and that, conversely, no end-use is going to be linked to any one product or service.

Some implications of this are that increasingly the *noncustomers* of an enterprise—whether a business, a university, a church, a hospital—are as important as the customers, if not more important.

Even the biggest enterprise (other than a government monopoly) has many more noncustomers than it has customers. There are very few institutions that supply as large a percentage of a market as 30 percent. There are therefore few institutions where the noncustomers do not amount to at least 70 percent of the potential market. And yet very few institutions know anything about the noncustomers—very few of them even know that they exist, let alone know who they are. And even fewer know why they are not customers. Yet it is with the noncustomers that changes always start.

Another critical implication is that the starting point for management can no longer be its own product or service, and not even its known market and its known end-uses for its products and services. The starting point has to be what *customers consider value*. The starting point has to be the assumption—an assumption amply proven by all our experience—that the customer never buys what the supplier sells. What is value to the customer is always something quite different from what is value or quality to the supplier. This applies as much to a business as to a university or to a hospital.

One example is the pastoral mega-churches that have been growing so very fast in the United States since 1980, and that are surely the most important social phenomenon in American society in the last thirty years. Almost unknown thirty years ago—there were no more than a thousand churches then that had a congregation exceeding two thousand people—there are now some twenty thousand of them. And while all the traditional denominations have steadily declined, the mega-churches have exploded. They have done so because they asked, "What is value?" to a *nonchurchgoer*. And they have found that it is different from what churches traditionally thought they were supplying. The greatest value to the thousands who now throng the mega-churches—and do so weekdays and Sundays—is a spiritual experience rather than a ritual, and equally management responsibility for volunteer service, whether in the church itself or, through the church, in the community.

Management, in other words, will increasingly have to be based on the assumption that neither technology nor end-use is a foundation for management policy. They are **limitations.** *The foundations have to be customer values and customer decisions on the distribution of their disposable income. It is with those that management policy and management strategy increasingly will have to start.*

V
Management's Scope Is **Legally** *Defined*

Management, both in theory and in practice, deals with the legal entity, the individual enterprise—whether the business corporation, the hospital, the university and so on. The scope of management is thus *legally* defined. This has been—and still is—the almost universal assumption.

One reason for this assumption is the traditional concept of management as being based on command and control. Command and control are indeed legally defined. The chief executive of a business, the bishop of a diocese, the administrator of a hospital have no command and control authority beyond the legal confines of their institution.

Almost a hundred years ago it first became clear that the legal definition was not adequate to manage a major enterprise.

The Japanese are usually credited with the invention of the "Keiretsu," the management concept in which the suppliers to an enterprise are tied together with their main customer, for example, Toyota, for planning, product development, cost control and so on. But actually the Keiretsu is much older and an American invention. It goes back to around 1910 and to the man who first saw the potential of the automobile to become a major industry, William C. Durant (1861–1947). It was Durant who created General Motors by buying up small but successful automobile manufacturers such as Buick and merging them into one big automobile company. A few years later Durant then realized that he needed to bring the main suppliers into his corporation. He began to buy up and merge into General Motors one parts and accessories maker after the other, finishing in 1920 by buying Fisher Body, the country's largest manufacturer of automobile bodies. With this purchase General Motors had come to own the manufacturers of 70 percent of everything that went into its automobiles—and had become by far the world's most integrated large business. It was this prototype Keiretsu that gave General Motors the decisive advantage, both in cost and in speed, which made it within a few short years both the world's largest and the world's most profitable manufacturing company, and the unchallenged leader in an exceedingly competitive American automobile market. In fact, for some thirty-odd years, General Motors enjoyed a 30 percent cost advantage over all its competitors, including Ford and Chrysler.

But the Durant Keiretsu was still based on the belief that management means command and control—this was the reason that Durant *bought* all the companies that became part of General Motors' Keiretsu. And this eventually became the greatest weakness of GM. Durant had carefully planned to ensure the competitiveness of the GM-owned accessory suppliers. Each of them (excepting Fisher Body) had to sell 50 percent of its output outside of GM, that is, to competing automobile manufacturers, and thus had to maintain competitive costs and competitive quality. But after WWII the competing automobile manufacturers disappeared—and with them the check on the competitiveness of GM's wholly owned accessory divisions. Also, with the unionization of the automobile industry in 1936–1937, the high labor costs of automobile assembly plants were imposed on General Motors' accessory divisions, which put them at a cost disadvantage that to this day they have not been able to overcome. That Durant based his Keiretsu on the assumption that management means command and control largely explains, in other words, the decline of General Motors in the last twenty-five years and the company's inability to turn itself around.

This was clearly realized in the 1920s and 1930s by the builder of the next Keiretsu, Sears Roebuck. As Sears became America's largest retailer, especially of appliances and hardware, it too real-

ized the necessity to bring together into one group its main suppliers so as to make possible joint planning, joint product development and product design, and cost control across the entire
economic chain. But instead of buying these suppliers, Sears
bought small minority stakes in them—more as a token of its
commitment than as an investment—and based the relationship
otherwise on contract. And the next Keiretsu builder—and probably the most successful one so far (even more successful than the
Japanese)—was Marks & Spencer in England, which, beginning in
the early 1930s, integrated practically all its suppliers into its own
management system, but exclusively through contracts rather
than through ownership stakes or ownership control.

It is the Marks & Spencer model that the Japanese, quite con-
sciously, copied in the 1960s.

Actually, the share of even the most highly integrated
enterprise in the total costs and the total results of the
entire process is quite small indeed. While General Motors
at its peak manufactured 70 percent of everything that
went into the finished automobile, it got only 15 percent
of what the ultimate consumer actually paid for a new car.
Fifty percent of the total went for distribution, that is, for
costs incurred after the finished car had left the General
Motors assembly plant. Another 10–15 percent of the
total were various taxes. And of the remaining 35 percent
of the total, one-half—another 17 percent—was still payments to outside suppliers. Yet no manufacturing company in history has dominated a larger share of the total
economic process than did GM at the period of its greatest success, that is, in the 1950s and 1960s. The share of
the typical manufacturing company in the costs and revenues of the economic process—that is, what the customer
ultimately pays—rarely amounts to as much as an almost
insignificant 10 percent of the total. Yet if management's
scope is *legally* defined, this is all the manufacturer typically has any information on—and all it can even *try* to
manage.

In every single case, beginning with General Motors, the Keiretsu, that is, the integration into one management system of enterprises that are linked economically rather than controlled legally, has given a cost advantage of at least 25 percent and more often 30 percent. In every single case it has given dominance in the industry and in the marketplace.

And yet the Keiretsu is not enough. It is still based on power. Whether it is General Motors and the small, independent accessory companies that Durant bought between 1915 and 1920, or Sears Roebuck, or Marks & Spencer, or Toyota—the central company has overwhelming economic power. The Keiretsu is not based on a partnership of equals. It is based on the dependence of the suppliers.

Increasingly, however, the economic chain brings together genuine *partners*, that is, institutions in which there is equality of power and genuine independence. This is true of the partnership between a pharmaceutical company and the biology faculty of a major research university. This is true of the joint ventures through which American industry got into Japan after WWII. This is true of the partnerships today between chemical and pharmaceutical companies and companies in genetics, molecular biology or medical electronics. These companies in the new technologies may be quite small—and very often are—and badly in need of capital. But they own independent technology. Therefore *they* are the senior partners when it comes to technology. They, rather than the much bigger pharmaceutical or chemical company, have a choice with whom to ally themselves. The same is largely true in information technology, and also in finance. And then neither the traditional Keiretsu nor command and control work.

What is needed, therefore, is a redefinition of the scope of management. *Management has to encompass the entire process.* For business this means by and large the economic process. But the biology department of the major research university does not see itself as an economic unit, and cannot be managed as such. In other institutions the process also has to be defined differently. Where we have gone furthest in trying to build management of the entire process is American health care. The HMO (health maintenance organization) is an attempt—a first and so far a very tentative, very debatable attempt—to bring the entire process of health care delivery under partnership management.

> *The new assumption on which management, both as a discipline and as a practice, will increasingly have to base itself is that the scope of management is not legal.*

> *It has to be **operational**. It has to embrace the entire process. It has to be focused on results and performance across the entire **economic chain**.*

VI
Management's Scope Is Politically *Defined*

It is still generally assumed in the discipline of management—and very largely still taken for granted in the practice of management—that the domestic economy, as defined by national boundaries, is the ecology of enterprise and management—and of nonbusinesses as much as of businesses.

This assumption underlies the traditional "multinational."

As is well known, before WWI, as large a share of the world's production of manufactured goods and of financial services was multinational as it is now. The 1913 leading company in any industry, whether in manufacturing or in finance, derived as large a share of its sales from selling outside its own country as it did by selling inside its own country. But insofar as it produced outside its own national boundaries, it produced within the national boundaries of another country.

One example:

The largest supplier of war matériel to the Italian Army during WWI was a young but rapidly growing company called Fiat in Turin—it made all the automobiles and trucks for the Italian Army. The largest supplier of war matériel to the Austro-Hungarian Army in WWI was also a company called Fiat—in Vienna. It supplied all the automobiles and trucks to the Austro-Hungarian Army. It was two to three times the size of its parent company. For Austria-Hungary was a much larger market than Italy, partly because it had a much larger population, and partly because it was more highly developed, especially in its Western parts. Fiat-Austria was wholly owned by Fiat-Italy. But except for the designs that came from Italy, Fiat-Austria was a separate company. Everything it used was made or bought in Austria. All products were sold in Austria. And every employee up to and including the CEO was an Austrian. When WWI came, and Austria and Italy became enemies, all the Austrians had to do, therefore, was to change the bank account of Fiat-Austria—it kept on working as it had all along.

Even traditional industries like the automotive industry or insurance are no longer organized that way.

Until recently General Motors' two European subsidiaries, Opel in Germany and Vauxhall in the UK, were separate companies, one producing in Germany and selling on the Continent, one producing and selling in the UK. Now GM has *one* European company, designing, producing and selling in all of Europe and run out of one European headquarters. GM-Europe also produces in South America and Asia—and also sells in the United States. GM-Europe increasingly also designs for the rest of General Motors Worldwide. In turn, General Motors USA increasingly designs and produces for GM-Europe and GM-Brazil, and so on. The worldwide insurance companies—the foremost of them today a German one, Allianz—are increasingly moving major activities, such as settling claims, and above all investment, into central facilities that do the work for all the group's businesses, wherever they are.

Post-WWII industries such as the pharmaceutical industry, or the information industries, are increasingly not even organized in "domestic" and "international" units as GM and Allianz still are. They are run as a worldwide system in which individual tasks, whether research, design, engineering, development, testing and increasingly manufacturing and marketing, are each organized "transnationally."

One large pharmaceutical company has seven labs in seven different countries, each focusing on one major area (e.g., antibiotics) but all run as one "research department" and all reporting to the same research director in headquarters. The same company has manufacturing plants in eleven countries, each highly specialized and producing one or two major product groups for worldwide distribution and sale. It has one medical director who decides in which of five or six countries a new drug is to be tested. But managing the company's foreign exchange exposure is totally centralized in one location for the entire system. The medical-electronics business of the (American) General Electric Company has three "headquarters," one in the United States, one in Japan, one in France, each in charge worldwide of one major technology area and the products based on it (e.g., imaging products such as traditional X-ray machines or the more recent ultrasound machines). And each of the three manufactures in a dozen or more countries with each plant supplying a few key parts for all the other plants throughout the world.

In the traditional multinational, economic reality and political reality were congruent. The country was the "business unit," to use today's term. In today's transnational—but increasingly, also, in the old multinationals as they are being forced to transform themselves—the country is only a "cost center." It is a complication rather than the unit for organization and the unit of business, of strategy, of production and so on. (But see Chapter Two for some of the resulting problems.)

Management and national boundaries are no longer congruent. The scope of management can no longer be politically defined. National boundaries will continue to be important.

But the new assumption has to be:

National boundaries are important primarily as restraints. The practice of management—and by no means for businesses only—will increasingly have to be defined **operationally** *rather than* **politically.**

VII
The **Inside** *Is Management's Domain*

All the traditional assumptions led to one conclusion: *The inside of the organization is the domain of management.*

This assumption explains the otherwise totally incomprehensible distinction between management and entrepreneurship.

In actual practice this distinction makes no sense whatever. An enterprise, whether a business or any other institution, that does not innovate and does not engage in entrepreneurship will not survive long.

The oldest institution in the world is the Roman Catholic church. It is usually considered the most conservative one— and prides itself on not being given to rapid changes. Yet, as an old observation has it, any major change in society produces new and very different religious orders in the Roman Catholic church—the Benedictines in the 5th century A.D., when the Barbarians overran the Roman Empire; the Franciscans and Dominicans, seven hundred years later, when cities reemerged in the Middle Ages; the Jesuits in the 16th century as an answer to the Protestant Reformation, and so on. In Protestantism, as the great church historian Richard Niebuhr (1894–1962) showed in several books, any major change in society leads to the emergence of new Protestant denominations. The emergence of the Knowledge Society today, for instance, has led on the one hand to the explosive rise of the new, large, nondenominational, pastoral "mega-churches" that attract the new knowledge workers, and to equally explosive worldwide growth of Pentecostalism, attracting largely the less educated and therefore not upwardly mobile members of modern society.

It should have been obvious from the beginning that management and entrepreneurship are only two different dimensions of the same task. An entrepreneur who does not learn how to manage will not last long. A management that does not learn to innovate will not last long. In fact, as Chapter Three will argue, business—and every other organization today—has to be designed for change as the norm and to create change rather than react to it.

But entrepreneurial activities start with the Outside and are focused on the Outside. They therefore do not fit within the traditional assumptions of management's domain—which explains why they have come so commonly to be regarded as different, if not incompatible. Any organization, however, which actually believes that management and entrepreneurship are different, let alone incompatible, will soon find itself out of business.

The inward focus of management has been greatly aggravated in the last decades by the rise of Information Technology. Information Technology so far may actually have done more damage to management than it has helped, as discussed in greater depth in Chapter Four.

The traditional assumption that the inside of the organization is the domain of management means that management is assumed to concern itself with *efforts*, if not with *costs* only. For effort is the only thing that exists within an organization. And, similarly, everything inside an organization is a cost center.

But results of any institution exist only on the outside.

It is understandable that management *began* as a concern for the inside of the organization. When the large organizations first arose—with the business enterprise, around 1870, the first and by far the most visible one—managing the inside was the new challenge. Nobody had ever done it before. But while the assumption that management's domain is the inside of the organization originally made sense—or at least can be explained—its continuation makes no sense whatever. It is a contradiction of the very function and nature of organization.

Management must focus on the *results* and *performance* of the organization. Indeed, the first task of management is to define what results and performance are in a given organization—and this, as anyone who has worked on it can testify, is in itself one of the most difficult, one of the most controversial, but also one of the most important tasks. It is therefore the specific function of management to organize the resources of the organization *for results outside the organization*.

The new assumption—and the basis for the new paradigm on which management, both as a discipline and as a practice has to be based—is therefore:

> *Management exists for the sake of the institution's results.*
> *It has to start with the intended results and has to*
> *organize the resources of the institution to attain these*
> *results. It is the organ to make the institution, whether*
> *business, church, university, hospital or a battered*
> *women's shelter, capable of producing results outside of*
> *itself.*

Conclusion

This chapter has not tried to give answers—intentionally so. It has tried to raise questions. But underlying all of these is one insight. The center of a modern society, economy and community is not technology. It is not information. It is not productivity. *It is the managed institution as the organ of society to produce results.* And management is the specific tool, the specific function, the specific instrument to make institutions capable of producing results.

This, however, requires a *FINAL* new management paradigm:

> *Management's concern and management's responsibility*
> *are everything that affects the performance of the*
> *institution and its results—whether inside or outside,*
> *whether under the institution's control or totally beyond it.*

2

Strategy—The New Certainties

Introduction
Why Strategy?

*Every organization operates on a Theory of the Business,** that is, a set of assumptions as to what its business is, what its objectives are, how it defines results, who its customers are, what the customers value and pay for.

Strategy converts this Theory of the Business into performance. Its purpose is to enable an organization to achieve its desired results in an unpredictable environment. For strategy allows an organization to be *purposefully opportunistic*.

Strategy is also the test of the Theory of the Business. Failure of the strategy to produce the expected results is usually the first serious indication that the Theory of the Business needs to be thought through again. And unexpected successes are often also the first indications that the Theory of the Business needs to be rethought. Indeed, what is an "opportunity" can only be decided if there is a strategy. Otherwise, there is no way to tell what genuinely advances the organization toward its desired results, and what is diversion and splintering of resources.

But what can strategy be based on in a period of rapid change and total uncertainty, such as the world is facing at the turn of the 21st century? Are there any assumptions on which to base the strategies of an organization and especially of a business? Are there any *certainties*?

There are indeed FIVE phenomena that can be considered *certainties*. They are, however, different from anything present strategies consider. Above all, they are not, essentially, economic. They are primarily social and political.

These five certainties are:

1.   The Collapsing Birthrate in the Developed World.

2.   Shifts in the Distribution of Disposable Income.

---

*On this see "The Theory of the Business," Chapter One, *Peter Drucker on The Profession of Management* (Cambridge, Mass.: Harvard Business School Press, 1998).

3. Defining Performance.

4. Global Competitiveness.

5. The Growing Incongruence Between Economic Global-
   ization and Political Splintering.

I
The Collapsing Birthrate

The most important single new certainty—if only because there is
no precedent for it in all of history—is the *collapsing birthrate in the
developed world*. In Western and Central Europe and in Japan, the
birthrate has already fallen well below the rate needed to repro-
duce the population. That is, below 2.1 live births for women of
reproductive age. In some of Italy's richest regions, for example,
in Bologna, the birthrate by the year 1999 had fallen to 0.8; in
Japan to 1.3. In fact, Japan and all of Southern Europe—Portugal,
Spain, Southern France, Italy, Greece—are drifting toward collec-
tive national suicide by the end of the 21st century. By then Italy's
population, for instance—now 60 million—might be down to 20
or 22 million; Japan's population—now 125 million—might be
down to 50 or 55 million. But even in Western and Northern
Europe the birthrates are down to 1.5 and falling.

But in the United States, too, the birthrate is now below 2 and
going down steadily. And it is as high as it is only because of the
large number of recent immigrants who still, for the first generation, tend to retain the high birthrates of their country of origin,
for example, Mexico.

In Japan and in Southern Europe, population is already peak-
ing as it is in Germany. In the United States it will still grow for
another twenty to twenty-five years, though the entire growth
after the year 2015 will be in people fifty-five years and older.

But more important than absolute numbers is the age distribution within the population. Of those 20-odd million Italians
by the year 2080, a very small number will be under fifteen, and a
very large number—at least one-third of the population—well

above sixty. In Japan the disproportion between younger people and people above any traditional retirement age will be equally great if not greater. In the United States, the young population is already growing much more slowly than the older population, past traditional retirement. Still, up to the year 2015 or so, the number of young people will still be growing in absolute numbers in the United States. But then it is likely to go down and quite rapidly.

Birthrates can change, and can do so quite fast, as the American experience after World War II proved. But even if the birthrates in the developed world were to turn up drastically, it would take twenty years or so before these new babies would reach the age at which they join the labor force. There is nothing—except unprecedentedly massive immigration—that can prevent a sharp drop in the labor force of traditional age (i.e., below sixty or sixty-five) in the developed world—in the United States after 2025 or so, in the rest of the developed world much earlier.

There is no precedent for this. The birthrate within part of the Roman Empire may have been falling after A.D. 200 or 250 but, of course, there are no figures. Above all, there is no precedent for a population structure in which old people past any traditional retirement age outnumber young people as they already do in parts of Europe and as they will do in all developed countries well before the middle of the 21st century.

For at least two hundred years, all institutions of the modern world and especially all businesses have assumed a steadily growing population. In the West the population has been growing since 1400. And from 1700 on the growth has been very fast—until well after World War II. Population growth in Japan began around 1600 or so, that is, after the end of the Civil Wars. It speeded up around 1800 and has continued until well after World War II. But increasingly, in all developed countries, the strategy of all institutions will have to be based, from now on, on the totally different assumption of a *shrinking* population, and especially of a shrinking young population.

An aging population—the demographic phenomenon that now preoccupies economists, politicians and the public in all developed countries—is nothing new. Life expectancies have been growing in the developed world since the 18th and certainly since the 19th century. They have not even been growing very much faster the last fifty years than they did in the last hundred and fifty years. And we also know how to deal with the problem. It will be difficult, painful, turbulent and terribly unpopular, to be sure. But within the next twenty to thirty years the retirement age in all developed countries will have to move up to around seventy-nine or so—seventy-nine being the age that, in terms of both life and health expectancies, corresponds to age sixty-five in 1936, when the United States, the last Western country to do so, adopted a national retirement plan (Social Security).

Similarly, there is nothing particularly new in the growth of the population in the Third World. It largely parallels the growth of population in the developed countries a hundred years earlier—it is not even significantly faster. And the population growth in most of the Third World is slowing down so fast that one can predict with near certainty that population in the Third World—excepting perhaps only India—will level off well before it reaches a crisis point. We know that in terms of food and raw materials there is going to be no major crisis. We know that clean water and clean air will present tremendous problems—and that altogether population and environment will have to be brought into balance. But that too is not as new a problem as most people believe. In some places in Europe (e.g., the German Ruhr) the problem was faced early in the 20th century and was solved then, and quite satisfactorily.

What is, to repeat, totally unprecedented is the collapse of the birthrate in the developed world.

Some of the implications are clear.

(1) For the next twenty or thirty years demographics will dominate the politics of all developed countries. And they will inevitably be politics of *great turbulence*. No country is prepared for the issues. Indeed, in no country are political factions and political parties aligned around the issues that demographics pose. Is extending retirement age "right" or "left"? Is encouraging older people to keep on working past age sixty by exempting from taxes part or all of their earned income "progressive" or "reactionary," "Liberal" or "Conservative"?

But equally upsetting—perhaps even more so—will be the

political issue of immigration. The population decline in the developed and rich countries is accompanied by population growth in most of the neighboring and poor countries of the Third World—in the case of the United States, in Central America and the Caribbean; in the case of Southern Europe, in North Africa; in the case of Germany, a Third World Russia; in the case of Japan, the Philippines, Indonesia and mainland Southeast Asia. To prevent immigration pressure is, however, very much like preventing the law of gravity. Yet there is no more inflammatory issue than large-scale immigration, especially from countries of different cultures and religions. And the turbulence will, in all likelihood, be most severe in Japan, in part because it still has the lowest retirement age, in part because its labor market is totally inflexible, but also because Japan has never before—at least not in her recorded history—allowed any immigration whatsoever. Conversely, the problems are likely to be least severe in the United States both because it is, after all, a country of immigrants and because it has the most flexible labor markets. But even in the United States the demographic changes are bound to create enormous political emotions and to bring about totally new—and unpredictable—political shifts.

(2) For the next twenty or thirty years no developed country is likely, therefore, to have stable politics or a strong government. Government instability is going to be the norm.

(3) "Retirement" may come to mean two different things. It is quite likely that the trend toward "early retirement" will continue. But it will no longer mean that a person stops working. It will come to mean that a person stops working full-time or as an employee for an organization for the entire year rather than a few months at a time. Employment relations—traditionally among the most rigid and most uniform relationships—are likely to become increasingly heterogeneous and increasingly flexible, at least for older people (on this see also Chapters One and Six). This will increasingly be the case as the center of gravity in the older population shifts from manual workers to people who have never worked with their hands, and especially to knowledge workers—a shift that will begin in the United States around the year 2010 when the babies of the "baby boom" which began in 1948

reach traditional retirement age. For these babies were the first age cohort in human history, a majority of which did not go into manual work but increasingly into knowledge work. They are therefore also the first age cohort in human history who, after thirty or forty years of full-time work, are not physically worn out by hard manual labor but still, in the great majority, perfectly capable to function and to work, both physically and mentally.

Major innovations in work and employment are therefore already needed in Europe and Japan. In the United States there may still be enough young people to postpone radical changes until around 2010. Yet in all likelihood the new employment relations are likely to be developed first in the United States, again because it has the most flexible and least restrictive labor markets and a tradition of experimentation by individual employers as well as by individual employees.

In the United States, therefore, employing organizations—and by no means only businesses—should start as soon as possible to experiment with new work relationships with older people and especially with older knowledge workers. The organization that first succeeds in attracting and holding knowledge workers past traditional retirement age, and makes them fully productive, will have a tremendous competitive advantage. In any event the strategy of any organization should be based on the assumption that twenty or thirty years hence, a large and growing part of the work—including some of the organization's most important work—will be done by people who are past traditional working age; who are not and should be neither "executives" nor "subordinates," but have no rank; who, above all, are not "employees" in the traditional sense and certainly not full-timers coming to work in a corporate office every day.

(4) The final implication is that in all developed countries the productivity of all workers—whether full-time or part-time—and especially of all knowledge workers, will have to increase very rapidly (on this see Chapter Five). Otherwise the country—and every organization in it—will lose position and become steadily poorer.

But what are the implications for the individual company in a developed country?

The first question is whether the steady growth in the number of older people will continue to provide market opportunities—and for how long? In all developed countries older people have become the most prosperous group in the society, with their postretirement incomes in many cases substantially higher than their preretirement incomes. Their numbers will continue to increase. But will their income stay high or go down? And will they continue to spend as freely as they have been doing? And—the biggest question mark—will they continue to want to be "young" and spend accordingly? The answer to these questions will very largely shape the *consumer* market in the developed countries and with it the economy altogether.

And what does the shrinkage in the number of young people—and especially of people under eighteen, that is, babies, children and teenagers—mean for the economy and for the individual business? Is it only a threat? Or may it also be an opportunity for a particular institution?

That there will be fewer children might be seen as a tremendous opportunity for upgrading schools everywhere. So far, Japan is the only country that even understands that the crucial element in a country's ability to perform is the education of the small child, and that therefore the elementary school teacher is the truly important part of the educational establishment, and needs to be treated, to be respected and to be paid as such.

But even for a business that makes its living making goods for small children, the collapsing birthrate may be an opportunity. It is conceivable that having fewer children means that the child becomes more and more precious and that a larger share of the disposable income is spent on it.

This apparently has already happened in the one country that has had a shrinking birthrate as a national goal: China. The Chinese policy that restricts a family to one child has been quite effective in the large cities of China, where a majority of families have only one child. And there many families, despite their poverty, apparently spend more on the single child than they used to spend on three or four children. There are signs in Germany, but also in Italy, of similar developments. And even in the

United States the middle-class family—where the birth-rate is already way down—is clearly spending a good deal more on its fewer children. That it realized and exploited this underlay the tremendous success of the Mattel Company with its expensive Barbie dolls.

The birthrate collapse has tremendous political and social implications that we cannot even guess at today. But it surely will also have tremendous economic and business implications—and some of those can already be explored, some of them can already be tested. Above all, any strategy, that is, any commitment of present resources to future expectations—and this, to repeat, is what a strategy means—has to start out with demographics and, above all, with the collapsing birthrate in the developed world. Of all developments, it is the most spectacular, the most unexpected and one that has no precedent whatever.

II
The Distribution of Income

Shifts in the shares of disposable income are just as important as shifts in population, but usually even less attention is paid to them. And they are likely—indeed all but certain—to be as dramatic as the demographic changes during the first decades of the 21st century.

Businesses and industries have become highly conscious of their market standing. They all keep figures on their sales and know whether their sales go up or down. All of them know whether they grow in volume or not. But practically none knows the truly important figure: the *share* of the disposable income of their customers—whether other institutions and businesses or ultimate consumers—that is being spent on the products or services that they produce and sell. And practically no one knows whether the share goes up or down.

Shares in disposable income are the foundation of all *economic* information. In the first place, of all the outside information needed by a business (see on this Chapter Four), it is usually the most easily obtainable. It is usually also the most reliable foundation for strategy. For as a rule, trends in the distribution of disposable income that go to a certain product category or service category tend, once established, to persist for long periods of time. They are usually impervious even to the business cycle.

But for that reason, there are few more important changes for an institution than a change in the trend. And equally important is a change *within* the trend, that is, a *switch* from one kind of product or service within a category to another product or service within the same category.

And within the first decades of the 21st century there will be *both* changes in the trends and changes within the trend. Yet neither executives nor economists pay much attention to the distribution of the shares of disposable income. In fact, most are totally ignorant of them.

> Practically all economists and the great majority of business executives believe, for instance, that the great economic expansion of the 20th century was driven by *economic* forces. It was not; on the contrary, the share of disposable income allocated to *economic* satisfaction has steadily *dropped* during this century in all developed countries.

The four growth sectors during the 20th century were, respectively:

- Government

- Health Care

- Education

- Leisure

with Leisure probably taking as much of the enormous expansion of economic productivity and output as the other three together.

> In 1900 the great majority of people in the developed countries still worked at least sixty hours a week, fifty-one weeks

a year—with about eight holidays a year—and six days a week. By the end of the century the great majority works fewer than forty hours a week—thirty-four or thirty-five in Germany—and at most (in the United States) forty-seven weeks a year (i.e., with about twelve holidays per year) and five days a week—a drop from more than 3,000 hours a year to fewer than 1,500 hours in Germany and to 1,850 hours in the hardest-working developed country, the United States.

Of these four 20th-century growth sectors, Government probably has the greatest impact on the distribution of disposable income. Not because it is a major buyer or user of products and services; except in wartime even the biggest government is only a marginal consumer. But the main *economic* function of government in a developed country is to *redistribute* between 30 and 50 percent of the country's national income. Nothing else has therefore as great an impact on the distribution of shares of national income as changes in government policy.

The other three—Health Care, Education, Leisure—are all major users of products and services, that is, of material goods. But none of them provides material, and that means "economic," satisfactions.

And all four are not in the "Free Market," do not behave according to the economist's rules of supply and demand, are not particularly "price sensitive" and altogether do not fit the economist's model or behave according to the economist's theories.

And yet, together, they are well over half of a developed economy, even of the most "capitalist" one.

The trends of these four sectors are therefore the first thing strategy has to consider. And all four are certain to change greatly in the next decades.

Government in its traditional form, that is, as collector and redistributor of national income, is supposed to have stopped growing (though the figures so far, especially in the United States and the UK, do not support this belief). But governments in all developed countries—despite all "privatization"—are rapidly acquiring new and very powerful tools to influence—if not to control—the distribution of disposable income: new regulations that control and direct *economic* resources to new goals, for example, the environment. Strategy, therefore, has to consider government the first concern in industry or company strategy.

Leisure, by contrast, is "mature" and may be "declining." In the developed countries we are probably at the end of the steady cutting of weekly hours. Indeed, these are signs that work hours are going up again—especially in the United States and the UK. The leisure market—next to armaments the 20th century's fastest-growing market—already shows the signs of a declining market: rapidly increasing competition for *time*, that is, for the leisure market's "purchasing power"; sharply declining profit margins; and less and less true product differentiation, for example, between going to the movies or looking at a VCR on one's own TV at home.

Both health care and education should continue to be major "growth sectors"—demographics make reasonably sure of this. But both are certain to undergo major shifts within the sector, for example, the shift, discussed earlier, from schooling the young to the continued education of highly schooled adult knowledge workers. And, probably, the shifts in health care ahead of us—in every developed country—are going to be even more radical and may happen even faster.

What do these developments in the 20th century's growth sectors mean for the 21st century's strategy of an industry and of a particular institution within it, whether a business, a university, a hospital, a church?

The answer to this question first requires defining what makes an industry a "growth" industry, a "mature" industry or a "declining" industry. A growth industry is one in which the demand for its products, whether goods or services, grows faster than national income and/or population. An industry in which the demand for its products or services grows as fast as national income and/or population is a "mature" industry. And an industry in which the demand for its products or services grows less fast than national income and/or population is a "declining" industry, even if its absolute sales volume still continues to grow.

The passenger-automobile industry of the world, for instance, has been a declining industry for the last thirty or forty years. It was a growth industry until 1960 or perhaps 1970. By that time Europe and Japan had become fully motorized. Total sales of passenger cars the world over are still growing worldwide, though only slowly. But they are growing much less fast than either national income or population.

Similarly, since the First World War—and probably since 1900—the share of disposable income in the developed countries, but altogether in the world economy, that is being spent on commodities of all kinds has been going down steadily at the rate of one-half of one percent per annum compound—wartimes excepted. This has held true for both food and industrial raw materials. This has meant that since 1900, the prices of all commodities have trended downward over any period of time.

And the trend is still downward.

Mature or declining industries may turn around and again become growth industries.

This may be the case of industries that produce transportation materials, for example, locomotives or road-building equipment. In the developed countries the existing transportation infrastructure has been grossly undermaintained. In emerging and Third World countries it is decades behind the needs of the economy and of the population—with China, perhaps, the outstanding example. Will this lead to another transportation boom such as fueled the economic expansion of the mid-19th century? There are few signs of this so far—but it is one of the trends to be watched.

For, to repeat, few things are as important for a strategy—both as threat and as opportunity—as a change in the trend of the shares of disposable income that such an upturn would represent.

The Present Growth Industries

But what are the *present* growth industries—and what can we learn from them?

The world's fastest-growing and most prosperous industry in the closing thirty years of the 20th century has not been Information. It has been Financial Services—but Financial Services the like of which did not exist at any earlier time, that is, retail services to provide an affluent, aging population in the developed countries with financial products to provide retirement income. And the demographic changes discussed earlier in this chapter largely underlie these new financial services.

Increasingly in the developed countries the newly affluent middle-class people, and especially those who do not work with their hands but work as service or knowledge workers, realize when they reach age forty-five or fifty that the existing retirement provisions are unlikely to be adequate should they survive into old age. And thus, beginning with age forty-five or fifty these people begin to look for investments that will promise them financial security thirty years hence.

This new growth industry is, however, quite different from the traditional financial industry such as the "corporate banker," a J. P. Morgan for instance, a Citibank or a Goldman Sachs. The new investors are not primarily interested in "making money" or in "deals." Their main concern is to maintain what little money they have as a cushion for their retirement years. The institutions that understand this—mutual funds, pension-fund managers and a few, mostly new, brokerage houses—have prospered mightily, first in the United States, then in the UK, and increasingly in Continental Europe and in the Japanese markets.

Most of the traditional financial "giants" did not, however, understand that the very meaning of "financial services" has changed. They only saw that "finance" takes a larger—a much larger—share of the disposable income in the developed countries. They therefore rapidly expanded their traditional "corporate" services. But actually the share of these traditional financial services—major corporate loans or major public offerings of corporate securities—is *not* growing. In all likelihood it is shrinking, and quite fast. For this is primarily a market of *big* companies. The growth sector in every developed country—even Japan—in the last twenty years has, however, been mid-sized businesses, with the share of big business going down steadily. And mid-sized businesses typically are not customers for traditional "corporate" financial services.

As a result the traditional financial giants have greatly overexpanded worldwide. And as their legitimate corporate business became less and less profitable—in part because there was increasingly less of it, in part because competition for the pieces of the shrinking pie has become fiercer and fiercer, driving down profits to the vanishing point—these corporate-banking giants, American, British, Japanese, German, French, Swiss, have increasingly resorted to "trading for their own account," that is, to outright speculation, so as to support their swollen overheads. This, however, as centuries of financial history teach (beginning with the Medici in 15th-century Europe), has only one—but an absolutely certain—outcome: catastrophic losses. And it is these losses resulting from a misreading of the trend toward financial services as a major growth industry which in large measure triggered the financial crisis that began in Asia in the mid-nineties and is threatening to engulf the entire world economy.

The actual trend, that is, the growth of the new "retail finance" and of the new investors, is, however, likely to continue despite the crisis. At least it is likely to continue until developed societies have adapted their retirement systems to the new demographic realities discussed earlier in this chapter.

Here is another example—and another lesson.

Everybody knows that what we call "information"—and what might be more aptly called "Access to the World"—has been a major growth industry, growing much faster in every developed or developing country—and even in totally under-developed Third World countries—than either national income or population. All of us hear "Electronics" or "Computers" when we hear "Information." But the number of *printed books* published and sold in every developed country has gone up in the last thirty or forty years as fast as the sales of the new electronics (on this see Chapter Four). The world's leading book publishing companies may not have grown as fast as some of the top electronic companies such as Intel and Microsoft in the United States or SAP in Germany, but they have grown faster than the electronic-information industry in its totality—and are arguably more profitable. And yet, though the United States has been the world's biggest and fastest-growing printed-book market, no U.S. publisher saw this. As a result many American book publishers are now owned by non-Americans (with Bertelsmann, Holtzbrinck and Murdoch in the lead). And these firms increasingly dominate the printed-book market in the rest of the world—and it is growing there just as fast as in the United States, in Japan or in Europe (e.g., Bertelsmann's book clubs in China).

Industries, whether businesses or nonbusinesses, have to be managed differently depending on whether they are growth industries, mature industries or declining industries. A growth industry that can count on demand for its products or services growing faster than economy or population manages to create the future. It needs to take the lead in innovation and needs to be willing to take risks. A mature industry needs to be managed to have a leadership position in a few, a very few, but crucial areas, and especially in areas where the demand can be satisfied at substantially lower cost by advanced technology or advanced quality. And it needs to be managed for *flexibility* and *rapid change*. A mature industry shifts from one way of satisfying wants to another. A mature industry therefore needs to be managed for alliances, partnerships and joint ventures to adapt rapidly to such shifts.

One example is the pharmaceutical industry. Until very recently—since the invention of the sulfa drugs and the antibiotics just before World War II—it was a leading growth industry. In the 1990s it became a mature industry. This means with high probability that there will be fast and sudden shifts to new ways of satisfying the old demands, for example, from chemical drugs to genetics, molecular biology, medical electronics, or even to "alternative medicine."

In a declining industry one has to manage, above all, for steady, systematic, purposeful *cost reduction* and for steady improvement in *quality* and *service*, that is, for strengthening the company's position within the industry, rather than for growth in volume—which one can only take away from somebody else. For in a declining industry it is more and more difficult to establish meaningful product differentiation. Products in a declining industry tend to become "commodities"—as is rapidly happening with passenger automobiles (except so far for a few luxury cars).

In conclusion, institutions—businesses as well as nonbusinesses—will have to learn to base their strategy on their knowledge of, and adaptation to, the trends in the distribution of disposable income and, above all, to any shifts in this distribution. And they need both *quantitative* information and *qualitative* analysis.

III
Defining Performance

James Harrington (1611–1677), the Father of the English political philosophy out of which grew Locke, Hume, Burke, and *The Federalist Papers*, laid down in his book *Oceania* that "Power Follows Property." It was the shift in property from the great nobles to the country squires, he argued, that explained the English Revolution of the 1640s, the overthrow of absolute government and its replacement by the parliamentary government of the new property owners, the local gentry.

Demographics have, within the last fifty years, shifted property in all developed countries. We now are beginning to see the resultant shifts in power. Two developments—the emergence of an affluent (though by no means rich) middle class of nonmanual workers, and the extension of life expectancy—have led to the development of institutions such as the pension funds and the mutual funds. And these are now the legal "owners" of the key property in a modern, developed society, that is, of the publicly owned corporations.

The development began in the United States (it was first described in my 1975 book, *The Unseen Revolution*, reissued in 1993 as *The Pension Fund Revolution*). As a result, institutions representing the future pensioners now own at least 40 percent of all American publicly listed corporations, and probably more than 60 percent of the big ones. They similarly own British business. And they are beginning to be the owners of business in all other developed countries, Germany, France, Japan and so on. And with that shift in property, we are seeing a shift in power.

This underlies the present debate about the Governance of Corporations, which is basically a debate concerning for whose benefit businesses should be run. It underlies the dramatic shift to the predominance of the "shareholder interest." And a similar debate is beginning to emerge in all other developed countries.

Till now it has not been the prevailing theorem in any country that a business, and especially a large business, should be run exclusively—or even primarily—in the interest of the shareholders. In the United States, since the late 1920s, the prevailing theorem, however fuzzy, held that the business should be run for a balance of interests—customers, employees, shareholders and so on—which in fact meant that it should not be accountable to anyone. Britain more or less followed the same path. In Japan, Germany and Scandinavia, large enterprises have been seen—and are still being seen—as being run primarily to create and to maintain social harmony, which in effect means that they are to be run in the interest of manual workers.

These traditional views are now obsolescent. But the emerging American theorem that businesses should be run exclusively for the short-term interest of the shareholders is also not tenable, and will certainly have to be revised.

The future economic security of more and more people—that is, of the people who can expect to live into old age—is increasingly dependent on their *economic* investments—that is, on their income as owners. The emphasis on *performance* as that which most benefits the shareholders will therefore not go away. Immediate gains, whether in earnings or in share price, are, however, not what they need. They need economic returns twenty or thirty years hence. But at the same time, as Chapter Five on the productivity of the knowledge worker explains, businesses will increasingly have to satisfy the interests of their knowledge work employees—or at least put these interests high enough to attract and to hold the knowledge workers they need, and to make them productive.

Consequently, the employee for whose sake the traditional German or Japanese company is supposed to be run, that is, the manual worker, will increasingly be less and less important—and with it the traditional emphasis on "social harmony" as the performance objective of business enterprise, and especially of large enterprise.

The present debate about the Governance of Corporations is therefore only a first skirmish. We will have to learn to establish new definitions of what "performance" means in a given enterprise, and especially in the large, publicly owned enterprise. We will have to learn how to balance short-term results—which is what the present emphasis on "shareholder value" amounts to—with the long-range prosperity and survival of the enterprise. Even in purely financial terms, we face something totally new: the need for an enterprise to survive thirty or forty years, that is, to survive until its investors are reaching pensionable age. This is a formidable goal—and so far quite Utopian. The average life span of business enterprise, at least as a successful organization, has never in the past been more than thirty years. We will therefore have to learn to develop new concepts of what "performance" means in an enterprise. We will have to develop new measurements and so on. But at the same time performance will have to be defined nonfinancially so as to be meaningful to the knowledge workers and to generate "commitment" from them. And that is a nonfinancial, a "value" return.

All institutions will therefore have to think through what performance means. This used to be obvious and simple. It no longer is. And strategy increasingly will have to be based on new definitions of performance.

IV
Global Competitiveness

All institutions have to make *global competitiveness* a strategic goal. No institution, whether a business, a university or a hospital, can hope to survive, let alone to succeed, unless it measures up to the standards set by the leaders in its field, anyplace in the world.

One implication: It is no longer possible to base a business or a country's economic development on cheap labor. However low its wages, a business—except for the smallest and most purely local one, for example, a local restaurant—is unlikely to survive, let alone to prosper, unless its workforce rapidly attains the productivity of the leaders of the industry anyplace in the world. This is true particularly in manufacturing. For in *most* manufacturing industries of the developed world the cost of manual labor is rapidly becoming a smaller and smaller factor—one-eighth of total costs or less. *Low labor productivity* endangers a company's survival. But *low labor costs* no longer give enough of a cost advantage to offset low labor productivity.

This (as already said in Chapter One) also means that the economic development model of the 20th century—the model first developed by Japan after 1955 and then successfully copied by South Korea and Thailand—no longer works. Despite their enormous surplus of young people qualified only for unskilled manual work, emerging countries from now on will have to base growth either on technological leadership (as did the United States and Germany in the second half of the 19th century), or on productivity equal to that of the world leaders in a given industry, if not on themselves becoming the world's productivity leaders.

The same is true for all areas: Design, Marketing, Finance, Innovation—that is, for management altogether. Performance below the world's highest standards stunts, even if the costs are very low and even if government subsidies are very high. And "Protection" no longer protects, no matter how high the custom duties or how low the import quotas.

Still, in all likelihood, we face a protectionist wave throughout the world in the next few decades. For the first reaction to a period of turbulence is to try to build a wall that shields one's own garden from the cold winds outside. But such walls no longer protect institutions—and especially businesses—that do not perform up to world standards. It will only make them more vulnerable.

The best example is Mexico, which for fifty years from 1929 on had a deliberate policy of building its domestic economy independent of the outside world. It did this not only by building high walls of protectionism to keep foreign competition out. It did it—and this was uniquely Mexican in the 20th-century world—by practically forbidding its own companies to export. This attempt to create a modern but purely Mexican economy failed dismally. Mexico actually became increasingly dependent on imports, both of food and of manufactured products, from the outside world. It was finally forced to open itself to the outside world, since it simply could no longer pay for the needed imports. And then Mexico found that a good deal of its industry could not survive.

Similarly, the Japanese tried to protect the bulk of their business and industry by keeping the foreigners out while creating a small but exceedingly competitive number of export industries—and then providing these industries with capital at very low or no cost, thus giving them a tremendous competitive advantage. That policy too has failed. The present (1999) crisis in Japan is in large part the result of the failure to make the bulk of Japanese business and industry (and especially its financial industries) globally competitive.

Strategy, therefore, has to accept a new fundamental. Any institution—and not just businesses—has to measure itself against the standards set by each industry's leaders anyplace in the world.

V
The Growing Incongruence Between Economic Reality and Political Reality

The final fundamental on which to base strategy in the period of worldwide structural change and uncertainty is the growing *incongruence* between economic reality and political reality.

The world economy is increasingly becoming global. National boundaries are impediments and cost centers. As discussed in the first chapter of this book, business—and increasingly many other institutions as well—can no longer define their scope in terms of national economies and national boundaries. They have to define their scope in terms of industries and services worldwide.

But at the same time, political boundaries are not going to go away. In fact, it is doubtful that even the new regional economic units, the European Economic Community, the North American Free Trade Zone (NAFTA) or Mercosur, the proposed economic community in South America, will actually weaken political boundaries, let alone overcome them.

There has been talk about the "end of sovereignty" since well before 1918. But nothing has emerged yet to take the place of national government and national sovereignty in political affairs. In fact, since 1914, the trend has been toward increasing splintering. Gone are the empires that politically unified the largest areas of the world before 1914—Austria-Hungary and the Ottoman Empire; the British, the French, the Dutch; the Portuguese and the Belgian Empires; the Eurasian Empire of Tsars and Communists. At the same time, small political units have become economically viable because money and information have become "transnational" (which actually means that they have no nationality whatever). Since 1950 one mini-state after the other has come into being, each with its own government, its own military, its own diplomatic service, its own tax and fiscal policy and so on. So far there are no signs yet of any *global* institutions, not even in the economic sphere, for example, a global Central Bank controlling the totally reckless flows of money worldwide, let alone a global institution controlling tax and monetary policies worldwide.

Even within transnational economic units, national politics still overrule economic rationality. Despite the European Economic Community, for instance, it has proven all but politically impossible to close a totally redundant plant in Belgium and shift the work to a French plant of the same company only thirty miles away, but on the other side of a national border.

We have in fact three overlapping spheres. There is a true global economy of money and information. There are regional economies in which goods circulate freely and in which impediments to the movement of services and of people are being cut back, though by no means eliminated. And then increasingly there are national and local realities, which are both economic, but above all political. And all three are growing fast. And businesses—and other institutions, for example, universities—have no choice. They have to live and perform in all spheres, and at the same time. This is the reality on which strategy has to be based. But no management anyplace knows yet what this reality actually means. They are all still groping.

Many—perhaps most—large multinationals in manufacturing, in finance, in insurance have organized themselves into worldwide "business units" across national boundaries. The leasing business of a financial services company is, for example, run as one business, whether in Spain or in Hong Kong. And it is run separately from any other business of the same financial services company in Spain or in Hong Kong, for example, the company's foreign exchange business. But company after company has learned that for the local government or the local labor union—or any other local political agency—the "business unit" is a meaningless fiction. For them Spain or Hong Kong are the only meaningful reality and the Spanish or Hong Kong businesses of the company are therefore the only units they perceive and accept and are willing to deal with. No company I know has yet been able to figure out in advance what decision and action can actually be handled as a decision or action of the "business unit" and which will have to be handled as a "national" one—let alone how to work out in advance how to make an action or a decision fit both realities, the economic reality of the transnational business unit and the political reality of Spanish or Hong Kong "sovereignty."

But some implications are already clear. First, it is clear *what not to do*—that is, to be willing to be bribed to subordinate economic decisions to local politics. Because the political unit is becoming increasingly less powerful economically, it is increasingly tempted to offer all kinds of bribes—exemption from taxes, for instance; special-tariff protection; a guaranteed monopoly; all kinds of subsidies, and so on—to obtain an economic advantage. A typical example is the lavish subsidies given to European and Japanese automobile companies by some Southeastern U.S. states to bribe the companies into putting their new U.S. plants into the state. But of course there are hundreds—and probably thousands—of additional examples.

And a good many of them are much worse examples. The European and Japanese automobile companies had good *economic* reasons (at least they thought so) to build plants in the United States. In many other cases—for instance the bribes offered by small countries—the bribe is the only reason for a company to go into a certain country or to bail out a local company in trouble. It is absolutely predictable, however, that a decision motivated by such a bribe rather than by economic reality will turn into a disaster.

This is what happened, for instance, to every single manufacturing plant put by a U.S. company in the 1960s and 1970s into a small Latin American country, because that country's government promised to give the company a monopoly in the national market.

"There ain't no bargains" is old folk wisdom. The first rule for a business in managing the incongruence between economic reality and political reality is therefore NOT to do anything that does not satisfy *economic* reality. The first question has to be: "If we didn't get the bribe, would we do this as part of our *business* strategy?" If the answer is "no," don't do it however tempting the bribe. It will be a costly failure. But even if the answer is "yes," it is almost certainly wise to say "no" to the proffered bribe. All experience—and there is plenty of it—indicates that, in the end, one pays and pays heavily for accepting such bribes.

Closely related is another "Don't." Do not expand or grow globally by going into businesses—especially not by acquisition—unless they fit into the company's Theory of the Business and its overall strategy.

In different regions or different countries, different products and/or services will behave differently. In France, for instance, the Coca-Cola Company does far better selling fruit juices than it does selling carbonated Cokes. In Japan one of its major products is coffee dispensed in vending machines. But both fruit juices and prepared coffee fit Coca-Cola's Theory of the Business and its strategy. Physically they are different from the original Coke. In every other aspect, that is, as businesses, they are exactly the same.

To repeat something said earlier in this chapter: A strategy enables an institution to be *purposefully opportunistic*. If what looks like an opportunity does not advance the strategic goal of the institution, it is not an opportunity. It is a distraction. Even if it fits—or seems to fit—a particular *national*, that is, political, reality, it is still a distraction and is to be left alone. Otherwise it is practically bound to end in failure.

So much for the "Don'ts." And now the two "Do's" we already know.

Business growth and business expansion in different parts of the world will increasingly not be based on mergers and acquisitions or even on starting new, wholly owned businesses there. They will increasingly have to be based on alliances, partnerships, joint ventures and all kinds of relations with organizations located in other political jurisdictions. They will, in other words, increasingly have to be based on structures that are economic units and not legal—and therefore not political—units.

There are many other reasons—some of them discussed earlier—that growth henceforth will be based on partnerships of all sorts rather than on outright ownership and command and control. But in all likelihood one of the most compelling ones will be the need to operate in both a global world economy and a splintered world polity. A partnership is by no means a perfect solution to this problem. In fact, partnerships have enormous problems of their own. But at least the conflict between economic reality and legal reality is greatly lessened if the economic unit is not also a legal unit, but is a partnership, an alliance, a joint venture that is a relationship in which political and legal appearance can be separated from economic reality.

The final implication: All businesses will have to learn to manage their currency exposure. Every business, even a purely local one, is in the world economy today. As such, it is subject to currency fluctuations even if it does not sell outside its own country, or does not buy outside it.

Even the most provincial and most local Mexican company was severely hit by the sudden collapse of the Mexican peso a few years ago. Even the most purely local Indonesian company was severely hit by the sudden collapse of the Indonesian currency in 1998.

There is no country today that is immune to sudden currency fluctuations—for the simple reason that the world is awash in "virtual money," that is, in liquidity for which there is no profitable investment. Every country, therefore, is awash in money that is not invested in property, in businesses, in manufacturing or in service enterprises, but kept in liquid and volatile "portfolio" investment. And very few countries have enough of a surplus in their balance of payments to service the interest on this "portfolio investment," let alone to pay it out should it take flight. Every country's currency, in other words, is at the mercy of short-term movements of money for which there may not be any economic rationale whatever.

This is the exact opposite of what was expected in 1973 when President Nixon cut the dollar loose from any fixed value and made it "float." The idea then was that this would limit currency fluctuations to minor adjustments. But because governments—beginning with the American government—grossly abused this new "freedom," currencies have become extremely unstable. They can be expected to continue to remain unstable. There is practically no reason to expect that the political units, that is, the various nations, will subordinate their fiscal, monetary and credit policies to any but their own political authority. It is to be hoped that the new European Bank will be able to maintain the Euro stable as a regional currency. But it is much too much to hope that the individual countries within the European unions will then subordinate their domestic policies to the stability of the Euro.

In other words, strategy has to be based on the assumption that currencies will continue to be volatile and unstable. One implication of this is that every management will have to learn what so far few managements can do: manage their foreign exchange exposure.

The realities discussed in this chapter do not tell an institution what to do, let alone how to do it. They raise the *questions* to which strategy has to find the answers for the individual institution. And there are questions that strategy so far has rarely, if ever, considered. But unless an institution starts out by considering these new realities, it will not have a strategy. It will not be prepared for the challenges that the next few years, if not the next few decades, are certain to raise. Unless these challenges can be met successfully, no enterprise can expect to succeed, let alone to prosper, in a period of turbulence, of structural change and of economic, social, political and technological transformation.

3

The Change Leader

Introduction
One Cannot Manage Change

One cannot *manage* change. One can only be ahead of it.

We do not hear much anymore about "overcoming resistance to change," which ten or fifteen years ago was one of the most popular topics of management books and management seminars. Everybody has accepted by now that "change is unavoidable." But this still implies that change is like "death and taxes": It should be postponed as long as possible, and no change would be vastly preferable.

But in a period of upheavals, such as the one we are living in, change is the norm. To be sure, it is painful and risky, and above all it requires a great deal of very hard work. But unless it is seen as the task of the organization to *lead change*, the organization—whether business, university, hospital and so on—will not survive. In a period of rapid structural change, the only ones who survive are the *Change Leaders*.

It is therefore a central 21st-century challenge for management that its organization become a change leader. A change leader sees change as opportunity. A change leader looks for change, knows how to find the right changes and knows how to make them effective both outside the organization and inside it. This requires:

1. Policies to make the future.

2. Systematic methods to look for and to anticipate change.

3. The right way to introduce change, both within and outside the organization.

4. Policies to balance change and continuity.

It is with these four requirements for being a change leader that this chapter concerns itself.

I
Change Policies

There is a great deal of talk today about "the innovative organization." But making an organization more receptive to innovation—even organizing it for innovation—is not nearly enough to be a change leader. It might even be a distraction. For to be a change leader requires the willingness and ability to change what is already being done just as much as to do new and different things. It requires policies to make the present create the future.

The first policy—and the foundation for all the others—is to *abandon yesterday*. The first need is to free resources from being committed to maintaining what no longer contributes to performance, and no longer produces results. In fact, it is not possible to create tomorrow unless one first sloughs off yesterday. To maintain yesterday is always difficult and extremely time-consuming. To maintain yesterday therefore always commits the institution's scarcest and most valuable resources—and above all, its ablest people—to nonresults. Yet to do anything different—let alone to innovate—always runs into unexpected difficulties. It therefore always demands leadership by people of high and proven ability. And if these people are committed to maintaining yesterday, they are simply not available to create tomorrow.

The first change policy, therefore, throughout the entire institution, has to be *Organized Abandonment*.

The change leader puts every product, every service, every process, every market, every distribution channel, every customer and end-use, on trial for its life. And it does so on a regular schedule. The question has to be asked—and asked seriously—"If we did not do this already, would we, knowing what we now know, go into it?" If the answer is "no," the reaction must not be "Let's make another study." The reaction must be "What do we *do* now?" The enterprise is committed to change. It is committed to *action*.

In three cases the right action is always outright abandonment.

Abandonment is the right action if a product, service,

market or process "still has a few good years of life." It is these dying products, services or processes that always demand the greatest care and the greatest efforts. They tie down the most productive and ablest people. But also we almost always overestimate how much "life" there is still in the old product, service, market or process. Usually they are not "dying"; they are dead. And as an old medical proverb has it, "There is nothing as difficult and as expensive, but also nothing as futile, as to try to keep a corpse from stinking."

But equally a product, service, market or process should be abandoned if the only argument for keeping it is: "It's fully written off." To treat assets as being fully written off has its place in tax accounting, but nowhere else. For *management* purposes there are no "cost-less assets." There are only "sunk costs," the economist's term for buildings and other fixed investments. The question is never: "What have they cost?" The question is: "What will they produce?" And assets that no longer produce except in accounting terms, that is, assets which produce only because they appear not to "cost" anything, are not assets. There are only sunk costs.

The third case where abandonment is the right policy—and the most important one—is the *old* and declining product, service, market or process for the sake of maintaining which, the *new* and growing product, service or process is being stunted or neglected.

One recent example of what not to do is how the future was sacrificed in the nineties, on the altar of yesterday, by America's largest automobile manufacturer, General Motors, and America's largest union of factory workers, the United Automobile Workers Union (UAW).

Everybody in the United States knows that the Japanese automobile makers acquired 30 percent of the U.S. passenger-car market in ten short years from the mid-seventies to the mid-eighties. But few realize that none of this gain was at the expense of America's two smaller manufacturers, Ford and Chrysler—on the contrary, both actually gained market share. One-third of the Japanese gain was at the expense of Germany's Volkswagen, which had a market share of 10 percent in the seventies but had lost practically all of it ten years later to the Japanese. Two-thirds of the Japanese gain—a hefty 20 percent of the American market—was, however, General Motors' loss; its market share slumped from 50 percent to 30 percent.

For fifteen years General Motors did nothing except fiddle with prices and discounts—none to any effect. Then, finally, in the late 1980s it decided to counterattack—with a new car called the "Saturn." The Saturn is little but a slightly more costly imitation of the Japanese—in its styling, its manufacturing and marketing, its service and its labor relations. And GM badly bungled its market introduction. Still it was a smash hit since a great many people in the United States were hungry for an American-made car of the new kind.

But, as almost everyone outside GM immediately realized, the Saturn did not compete with the Japanese makes. All its sales came at the expense of declining—if not dying—GM brands such as Oldsmobile and Buick. And then GM—and even more so GM's labor union, the United Automobile Workers—began to throttle the Saturn. It was denied money for expansion—that money went instead into futile attempts to "modernize" Oldsmobile and Buick plants. It was denied money to develop new models—again that money went into Oldsmobile and Buick redesigns. And the UAW began to whittle away at the Saturn's new and successful labor relations for fear that Saturn's example in building management-labor partnerships might spread to GM's other plants.

Neither Oldsmobile nor Buick has benefited. Both are still going downhill. But the Saturn has been all but destroyed. And both GM and the UAW have continued their decline.

. . .

Abandonment may take different forms.

In the GM cases, for instance, one possible solution might have been to do simultaneously two things: (1) kill the dying Oldsmobile and (2) run with Saturn's success as hard as possible, give it all the money and people it needed but set it up as a separate company free to compete aggressively with all of GM's old products and for all of GM's old customers.

The right answer may even be to do more of the same but to do it differently.

One example: Every book publisher knows that the bulk of its sales (some 60 percent)—and practically all of its profits—come from the "backlist," that is, from titles that have been out more than a year or two. But no book publisher puts resources into selling the backlist. All the efforts are put into selling the new titles. A major publishing firm had tried for years to get its salespeople to sell the backlist without any success; and it also did not itself spend a penny on promoting it. Then one outside director asked: "Would we handle the backlist the way we do if we went into it now?" And when the answer was a unanimous "no," she asked: "What do we *do* now?" As a result the firm reorganized itself into two separate units: one buying, editing, promoting and selling the new titles published in the current year; one promoting and selling the backlist. Within two years backlist sales had almost tripled—and the firm's profits doubled.

How to act on abandonment is thus the *second question*. It is as important as the first one. It is actually more controversial and more difficult. The answer should therefore always be tested on a small scale or *piloted* (see a later section of this chapter).

In a period of rapid change the "How?" is likely to become

obsolete faster than the "What?" The change leader must therefore also ask of every product, service, market or process: "If we were to go into this now, knowing what we now know, would we go into it the way we are doing it now?" And this question needs to be asked of the successful product, service, market and process as regularly—and as seriously—as of the unsuccessful product, service, market or process.

This applies to all areas of the enterprise. But it applies with particular force to an area that many enterprises tend to neglect, if not to ignore: distributors and distribution channels. In a time of rapid change distributors and distribution channels tend to change faster than anything else. And it is also on distributors and distribution channels that the "Information Revolution" is likely to have the greatest impact.

The terms "distributors" and "distribution channels" are of course business terms. But every institution has "distributors." And they are every institution's first "customers."

Here is a nonbusiness example:

> The high school placement counselor has been the "distribution channel" through whom American universities and colleges have traditionally reached prospective applicants for admission. But increasingly potential students and their parents look for information to ratings of colleges and universities published in a number of magazines, to books describing and rating different colleges and so on. Several major American universities have substantially increased the quantity and the quality of their applicants by focusing their promotional efforts on these new distribution channels—without necessarily cutting back on "selling" to the high school placement counselor.

> Similarly, the health maintenance organization (HMO) has increasingly become the "distribution channel" for hospitals, where, only ten years ago, the hospital distribution channel was the physician. Increasingly, hospitals are therefore working with HMOs to reach both physician and patient.

So far, we can only speculate on the impact the Internet will have on distribution. But it will have impact. One example of what is already happening, and happening fast, is the American automobile market.

It has been known for a long time that the wife makes the decision about what cars *not* to buy. She, in effect, therefore makes the buying decisions. But the wife, as has also been known for a long time, does not like to shop at the automobile dealer. Hence, it is the husband who appears as the buyer when the couple visits the dealer—even though the actual decision has already been made, and made by the wife. The Internet enables the woman to do the actual buying—the dealer is rapidly becoming no more than an "outlet."

Hence the automobile industry faces the task of making the Internet its distribution channel—General Motors is known already to work on this. But does that mean abandoning the traditional automobile dealer?

"To Abandon What" and "To Abandon How" have to be practiced systematically. Otherwise they will always be "postponed," for they are never "popular" policies.

Here is an example of how *successful* abandonment policies can be organized.

In one fairly big company offering outsourcing services in most developed countries, the first Monday morning of every month is set aside for an abandonment meeting at every management level from top management to the supervisors in each area. Each of these sessions examines one part of the business—one of the services one Monday, one of the regions in which the company does business a month later, the way this or that service is organized the Monday morning of the third month and so on. Within the year, the company this way examines itself completely, including its personnel policies, for instance. In the course of a year three to four major decisions are likely to be made on the "what" of the company's services and perhaps twice as many decisions to change the "how." But also each year three to five ideas for *new things* to do come out of these sessions. These decisions to change anything—whether to abandon something, whether to abandon the way something is being done or whether to do something new—are reported each month to all members of management. And twice a year all management levels report on what has actually happened as a result of their sessions, what action has been taken and with what results.

Since this company first began organized abandonment eight or nine years ago, it has grown more than four-fold (adjusted for inflation). It attributes at least half of this growth to its systematic abandonment policies.

Organized Improvement

The next policy for the change leader is *organized improvement* (what the Japanese call "Kaizen").

Whatever an enterprise does internally and externally needs to be improved systematically and continuously: product and service, production processes, marketing, service, technology, training and development of people, using information. And it needs to be improved at a preset annual rate: In most areas, as the Japanese have shown, an annual improvement rate of 3 percent is realistic and achievable.

However, continuing improvement requires a major decision. What constitutes "performance" in a given area? If performance is to be improved—and that is, of course, what continuous improvement aims at—we need to define clearly what "performance" means.

One example: complex and difficult products in which the rejection rate is high. To improve a rejection rate of 40 percent of a finished product to one of 35 percent is quite obviously a substantial improvement. But in most other areas the decision is by no means that simple. What is "quality" in a product? To what extent is it defined by the producer? To what extent can it only be defined by the customer? Even more difficult very often is the definition of performance in services.

Another example:

A major commercial bank decided that the way to improve performance in its branches was to offer new and more advanced financial "products," for example, selling Treasury bonds or giving advice on handling debt. It spent a great deal of time and money researching what kinds of financial products customers might want, developing these products and training its branch personnel to deliver them. But when the bank introduced the new products in its branches, it rapidly lost customers. Only then did the bank find out that to customers, performance of a bank branch means not having to wait in line for routine transactions. The additional "products" were valuable, the customers thought, but they only needed them once in a while.

The bank's solution was to concentrate the tellers at the branches on the simple, repetitive, routine services, which require neither skill nor time. The new financial products were assigned to different groups of people who were moved to separate tables, with big signs advertising the products in which each table specialized. As soon as this was done, business went up sharply, both for the traditional and the new services. But because there had been no "pilot"—trying out the improvements in one or two branches would have sufficed—the bank lost almost two years and a great deal of money.

Continuous improvements in any area eventually transform the operation. They lead to product innovation. They lead to service innovation. They lead to new processes. They lead to new businesses. Eventually continuous improvements lead to fundamental change.

Exploiting Success

The next policy that the change leader needs to develop is the *exploitation of success.*

It is only seventy or eighty years since the "monthly report" was invented and introduced in most business organizations. By now it is routine and standard practically everywhere. Almost without exception this report, on its first page, presents the areas in which results fall below expectations, or in which expenditures exceed budget. It focuses on problems. In the monthly operating committee meeting, which also has become routine and standard in practically all enterprises—and by no means only in businesses—it is this report on the problems that is being discussed, and nothing else.

Problems cannot be ignored. And serious problems have to be taken care of. But to be change leaders, enterprises have to *focus on opportunities. They have to starve problems and feed opportunities.*

This requires a small but fundamental procedural change: an additional "first page" to the monthly report, and one that should precede the page that shows the problems. It requires a page that focuses on where results are *better* than expected, whether in terms of sales, revenues, profits or volume. As much time then should be spent on this new first page as has traditionally been spent on the problem page. In some organizations that have successfully organized themselves to be change leaders, the opportunity page is given its own full morning or its own full day, with a second full morning or full day then devoted to the problems.

Enterprises that succeed in being change leaders make sure that they staff the opportunities.

The way to do this is to list the opportunities on one page, and then to list the organization's performing and capable people on another page. Then one allocates the ablest and most performing people to the top opportunities.

This implies that the first—and usually the best—opportunity for successful change is to exploit one's own successes and to build on them.

The best example, perhaps, is the Japanese company Sony. It has built itself into one of the world's leaders in a number of major businesses by systematically exploiting one success after the other—big or small.

All of Sony's consumer electronics—the business in which it is the world leader and best known—are based on a product that was not even invented by Sony: the tape recorder. One success of a Sony product based on the tape recorder is used to design the next product and then another product based on the success of that product and so on. No step was a big one. And not all of them were successful. But by exploiting success, each of these additional new products carried very little risk—so that even when it did not succeed there was not too much damage. And enough of them were successful to make Sony into one of the world's largest, but also one of the world's most consistently successful, enterprises.

Another example is the medical electronics group of the American General Electric Company. In a highly competitive field it has emerged as the largest and most successful manufacturer, but also as a change leader. It has done so apparently by exploiting its successes, and by building on each success another product—often with only a fairly minor change, but one that presents a significant improvement for physician or hospital.

As in a continuous improvement, exploitation will, sooner or later, lead to genuine innovation. There comes a point when the small steps of exploitation result in a major, fundamental change, that is, in something that is genuinely new and different.

II
Creating Change

The last policy for the change leader to build into the enterprise is a systematic policy of INNOVATION, that is, a policy to *create change*.

It is the area to which most attention is being given today. It may, however, not be the most important one—organized abandonment, improvement, exploiting success may be more productive for a good many enterprises. And without these policies—abandonment, improvement, exploitation—no organization can hope to be a successful innovator.

But to be a successful change leader an enterprise has to have a policy of *systematic innovation*. And the main reason may not even be that change leaders need to innovate—though they do. The main reason is that a policy of systematic innovation produces the mindset for an organization to be a change leader. It makes the entire organization see *change as an opportunity*.

Windows of Opportunity

This requires a systematic policy to look, every six to twelve months, for changes that might be opportunities—in the areas that I call "the windows of opportunity":

- The organization's own unexpected successes and unexpected failures, but also the unexpected successes and unexpected failures of the organization's competitors.

- Incongruities, especially incongruities in the process, whether of production or distribution, or incongruities in customer behavior.

- Process needs.

- Changes in industry and market structures.

- Changes in demographics.

- Changes in meaning and perception.

And finally:

- New knowledge.*

A change in any one of these areas raises the question: "Is this an *opportunity* for us to *innovate*, that is, to develop different products, services, processes? Does it indicate new and different markets and/or customers? New and different technologies? New and different distribution channels?" Innovation can never be risk-free. But if innovation is based on exploiting what has already happened—in the enterprise itself, in its markets, in knowledge, in society, in demographics and so on—it is far less risky than not to innovate by exploiting these opportunities.

Innovation is not "flash of genius." It is hard work. And this work should be organized as a regular part of every unit within the enterprise, and of every level of management.

What Not to Do

There are *Three Traps* to avoid into which change leaders fall again and again.

1. The first trap is an innovation opportunity that is not in tune with the strategic realities discussed in Chapter Two of this book.

   It is most unlikely to work. The only innovation likely to succeed is one that fits these major realities—of demo-

---

*These windows are described in considerable detail and with numerous examples in my 1985 book *Innovation and Entrepreneurship* (New York: HarperCollins; Oxford: Butterworth/Heinemann).

graphics, of the changes in the distribution of income, of the way the institution itself and its customers define "performance," of global competitiveness or of political and economic realities. But the "misfit" opportunity often looks very tempting—precisely because it looks truly "innovative." But even if not resulting in failure—as it usually does—it always requires extraordinarily wasteful amounts of effort, money and time.

2. The second trap is to confuse "novelty" with "innovation." The test of an innovation is that it creates value. A novelty only creates amusement. Yet, again and again, managements decide to innovate for no other reason than that they are bored doing the same thing or making the same product day in and day out. The test of an innovation—as is also the test of "quality"—is not: "Do we like it"? It is: "Do customers want it and will they pay for it?"

3. And the third trap: confusing motion with action. Typically when a product, service or process no longer produces results and should be abandoned or changed radically, management "reorganizes." To be sure, reorganization is often needed. But it comes *after* the action, that is, after the "what" and the "how" have been faced up to. By itself reorganization is just "motion" and no substitute for action.

These three traps are so attractive that every change leader can expect to fall into one of them—or into all three—again and again. There is only one way to avoid them, or to extricate oneself if one has stumbled into them: to organize the *Introduction of Change*, that is, to PILOT.

III
Piloting

Enterprises of all kinds increasingly use all kinds of market research and customer research to limit, if not eliminate, the risks of change. But one cannot market research the truly new. But also nothing new is right the first time. Invariably, problems crop up that nobody even thought of. Invariably, problems that loom very large to the originator turn out to be trivial or not to exist at all. Above all, the way to do the job invariably turns out to be different from what is originally designed. It is almost a "law of nature" that anything that is truly new, whether product or service or technology, finds its major market and its major application not where the innovator and entrepreneur expected, and not for the use for which the innovator or entrepreneur has designed the product, service or technology. And that, no market or customer research can possibly discover.

The best example is an early one.

The improved steam engine that James Watt (1736–1819) designed and patented in 1776 is the event which, for most people, signifies the advent of the Industrial Revolution. Actually, Watt until his death saw only one use for the steam engine: to pump water out of coal mines. That was the use for which he had designed it. And he sold it only to coal mines. It was his partner Matthew Boulton (1728–1809) who is the real father of the Industrial Revolution. Boulton saw that the improved steam engine could be used in what was then England's premier industry, textiles, and especially in the spinning and weaving of cotton. Within ten or fifteen years after Boulton had sold his first steam engine to a cotton mill, the price of cotton textiles had fallen by 70 percent. And this created both the first mass market and the first factory—and together modern capitalism and the modern economy altogether.

Neither studies nor market research nor computer modeling are a substitute for the *test of reality*. Everything improved or new needs therefore first to be tested on a small scale, that is, it needs to be PILOTED.

The way to do this is to find somebody within the enterprise who really wants the new. As said before, everything new gets into trouble. And then it needs a champion. It needs somebody who says: "I am going to make this succeed," and who then goes to work on it. And this person needs to be somebody whom the organization respects. This need not even be somebody within the organization. A good way to pilot a new product or new service is often to find a customer who really wants the new, and who is willing to work with the producer on making truly successful the new product or the new service.

If the pilot test is successful—if it finds the problems nobody anticipated but also finds the opportunities that nobody anticipated, whether in terms of design, of market, of service—the risk of change is usually quite small. And it is usually also quite clear where to introduce the change, and how to introduce it, that is, what entrepreneurial strategy to employ.

The Change Leader's Two Budgets

Finally, successful change leadership requires appropriate accounting and budget policies. It requires TWO separate budgets.

In most enterprises—and again not just in businesses—there is only one budget, and it is adjusted to the business cycle. In good times expenditures are increased across the board. In bad times expenditures are cut across the board. This, however, practically guarantees missing out on the future.

The change leader's first budget is an operating budget that shows the expenditures to maintain the present business. This is normally 80 to 90 percent or so of all expenditures.

That budget should always be approached with the question: "What is the *minimum* we need to spend to keep operations going?" And in poor times it should, indeed, be adjusted downward (though in good times most of it, probably, should not be adjusted upward, and certainly no more than volume and/or revenues increase).

And then the change leader has a second, separate budget for the future. This budget remains stable throughout good times and bad times. It rarely amounts to more than 10 or 12 percent of an enterprise's total expenditures—and again this applies to non-businesses as well as to businesses.

> Very few of the expenditures for the future produce results unless maintained at a stable level over substantial periods. This goes for work on new products, new services and new technologies; for the development of markets and customers and distribution channels, and above all, for the development of people.

The future budget should be approached with the question: "What is the *maximum* this activity can absorb to produce optimal results?" That amount should be maintained in good times or bad—unless times are so catastrophic that maintaining expenditures threatens the survival of the enterprise.

But the future budget also should include expenditures to exploit success. The most common, but also the most damaging, practice is to cut back on expenditures for successes, especially in poor times, so as to maintain expenditures for ongoing operations, and especially expenditures to maintain the past. The argument is always: "This product, service or technology is a success anyhow; it doesn't need to have more money put into it." But the right argument is: "This is a success, and therefore should be supported to the maximum possible." And it should be supported especially in bad times when the competition is likely to cut spending and therefore likely to create an opening.

We tend to manage according to the reports we receive and see. This explains why it is important for the change leader to have reports focusing on the areas in which the enterprise does better than expected, the areas of unexpected success, and therefore the areas of potential opportunity. It also explains why it is crucially important for the change leader to have a budget that embodies the commitment to making the future and to be ahead of change.

IV
Change and Continuity

The traditional institution is designed for continuity. All existing institutions, whether businesses, universities, hospitals or churches, therefore have to make special efforts to be receptive to change and to be able to change. It also explains why existing institutions face resistance to change. Change for the traditional institution is, so to speak, a contradiction in terms.

Change leaders are, however, designed for change. And yet they still require continuity. People need to know where they stand. They need to know the people with whom they work. They need to know what they can expect. They need to know the values and the rules of the organization. They do not function if the environment is not predictable, not understandable, not known. But continuity is equally needed outside the enterprise. In fact, we are learning increasingly the importance of long-term relationships. To be able to change rapidly, one needs close and continuous relationships with suppliers and distributors. But the enterprise also has to have a "personality" that identifies it among its customers and in its markets—and again this is true as much of nonbusinesses as of businesses.

Change and continuity are thus *poles* rather than opposites. The more an institution is organized to be a change leader, the more it will need to establish continuity internally and externally, the more it will need to *balance* rapid change and continuity.

This balance will predictably be one of the major concerns of tomorrow's management—both of the practitioners and of the scholars and writers on management. But we do know already a good deal about how to create it. Some institutions already are change leaders and have tackled the problem—though not always solved it.

One way is to make *partnership in change* the basis of *continuing* relationships. This is what the Japanese "Keiretsu" has done with respect to the relationship between supplier and manufacturer, and what is now adopted fast in American business through "Economic-Chain Accounting" (discussed in the next chapter of this book). We are developing similar partnerships in change as the basis of continuing relationships between manufacturer and distributor, for example, between Procter & Gamble, the world's largest producer of household needs, and large retailers such as Wal-Mart.

But relationships within the enterprise (as discussed earlier in Chapter One) are also increasingly going to be partnerships—with employees of the organization, with people who work for an out-sourcing firm but who are actually members of the enterprise's own working teams, or with outside, independent contractors. And again, these relations need increasingly to be organized as long-term partnerships in the process of change.

Balancing change and continuity requires continuous work on information. Nothing disrupts continuity and corrupts relationships more than poor or unreliable information (except, perhaps, deliberate misinformation). It has to become routine for any enterprise to ask at any change, even the most minor one: "Who needs to be informed of this?" And this will become more and more important as people no longer necessarily work next door to one another and see one another half a dozen times a day. The more enterprises come to rely on people working together without actually working *together*—that is, on people using the new technologies of information—the more important it will become to make sure that they are fully informed.

At the same time, it will also become more and more important for these people to get together and actually meet one another and work with one another on an organized, systematic, scheduled basis. Long-distance information does not replace face-to-face relationships. It makes them actually more important. It makes it more important for people to know what to expect of one another. It makes it more important for people to know how the other person actually behaves. It makes it more important to have trust in one another. And this means both systematic information—and especially information about any change—and organized face-to-face relationships, that is, opportunities to get to know one another and to understand one another.

Information is particularly important when the change is not a mere improvement, but something truly new. It has to be a firm rule in any enterprise that wants to be successful as a change leader, that there are *no surprises*. Above all, there is need for continuity in respect to the fundamentals of the enterprise: its mission, its values, its definition of performance and results. Precisely because change is a constant in the change leader's enterprise, the foundations have to be extra strong.

Finally, the balance between change and continuity has to be built into compensation, recognition and rewards. We long ago learned that an organization will not innovate unless innovators are properly rewarded. We long ago learned that a business in which successful innovators do not make it into senior management, let alone into top management, will not innovate. We will have to learn, similarly, that an organization will have to reward continuity—by considering, for instance, people who deliver continuing improvement to be as valuable to the organization, and as deserving of recognition and reward, as the genuine innovator.

V
Making the Future

One thing is certain for developed countries—and probably for the entire world: We face long years of profound changes. The changes are not primarily economic changes. They are not even primarily technological changes. They are changes in demographics, in politics, in society, in philosophy and, above all, in worldview. Economic theory and economic policy are unlikely to be effective by themselves in such a period. And there is no social theory for such a period either. Only when such a period is over, decades later, are theories likely to be developed to explain what has happened. But a few things are certain in such a period. It is futile, for instance, to try to ignore the changes and to pretend that tomorrow will be like yesterday, only more so. This, however, is the position that existing institutions tend to adopt in such a period—businesses as well as nonbusinesses. It is, above all, the policy likely to be adopted by the institutions that were most successful in the earlier period before the changes. They are most likely to suffer from the delusion that tomorrow will be like yesterday, only more so. Thus it can be confidently predicted that a large number of today's leaders in all areas, whether business, education or health care, are unlikely still to be around thirty years hence, and certainly not in their present form. But to try to anticipate the changes is equally unlikely to be successful. These changes are not predictable.

The only policy likely to succeed is to try to *make* the future. Changes of course have to fit the Certainties (which this book attempted to outline in the preceding chapter). Within these restraints, however, the future is still malleable. It can still be created.

To try to make the future is highly risky. It is less risky, however, than not to try to make it. A goodly proportion of those attempting to do what this chapter discusses will surely not succeed. But, predictably, no one else will.

4

Information Challenges

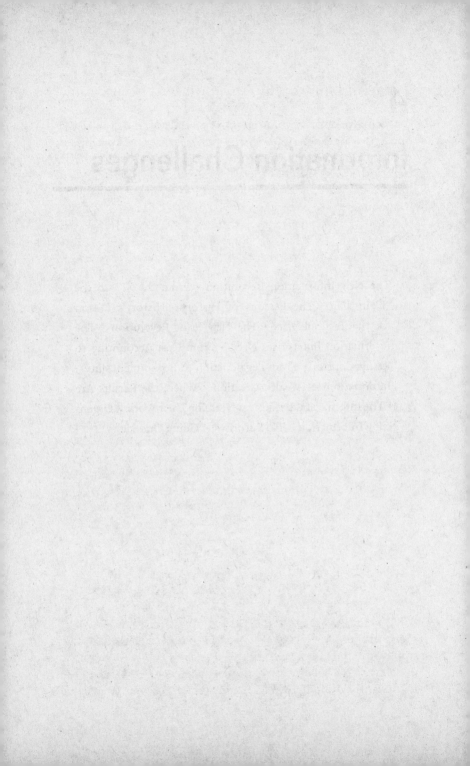

Introduction
The New Information Revolution

A new Information Revolution is well under way. It has started in business enterprise, and with business information. But it will surely engulf ALL institutions of society. It will radically change the MEANING of information for both enterprises and individuals. It is not a revolution in technology, machinery, techniques, software or speed. It is a revolution in CONCEPTS. It is not happening in Information Technology (IT), or in Management Information Systems (MIS), and is not being led by Chief Information Officers (CIOs). It is led by people on whom the Information Industry tends to look down: accountants. But an Information Revolution has also been going on in information for the individual. Again it is not happening in IT or MIS, and is not led by CIOs. It is a *print* revolution. And what has triggered these information revolutions and is driving them is the failure of the "Information Industry"—the IT people, the MIS people, the CIOs—to provide INFORMATION.

So far, for fifty years, Information Technology has centered on DATA—their collection, storage, transmission, presentation. It has focused on the "T" in "IT." The new information revolutions focus on the "I." They ask, "What is the MEANING of information and its PURPOSE?" And this is leading rapidly to redefining the tasks to be done with the help of information and, with it, to redefining the institutions that do these tasks.

I
From the "T" to the "I" in "IT"

A half century ago, around 1950, prevailing opinion overwhelmingly held that the market for that new "miracle," the computer, would be in the military and in scientific calculations, for example, astronomy. A few of us, however—a very few indeed—argued even then that the computer would find major applications in business and would have an impact on it. These few also foresaw—again very much at odds with the prevailing opinion (even of practically everyone at IBM, just then beginning its ascent)—that in business the computer would be more than a very fast adding machine doing clerical chores such as payroll or telephone bills. On specifics, we dissenters disagreed, of course, as "experts" always do. But all of us nonconformists agreed on one thing: The computer would, in short order, revolutionize the *work of top management*. It would, we all agreed, have its greatest and earliest impacts on business policy, business strategy and business decisions.

We could not have been more wrong. The revolutionary impacts so far have been where none of us then anticipated them: on OPERATIONS.

> Not one of us, for instance, could have imagined the truly revolutionary software now available to architects. At a fraction of traditional cost and time, it designs the "innards" of large buildings: their water supply and plumbing; their lighting, heating and air-conditioning; their elevator specifications and placement—work that even a few years ago still absorbed some two-thirds of the time and cost of designing an office building, a large school, a hospital or a prison.
>
> Not one of us could then have imagined the equally revolutionary software available to today's surgical residents. It enables them to do "virtual operations" whose outcomes include "virtually killing" patients if the resident makes the wrong surgical move. Until recently, residents rarely even saw much of an operation before the very end of their training.
>
> Half a century ago no one could have imagined the software that enables a major equipment maker such as Caterpillar to organize its operations, including manufacturing worldwide, around the anticipated service and replacement needs of its customers. And the computer has had a similar impact on bank operations, with banking probably the most computerized industry today.

But the computer and the information technology arising from it have so far had practically no impact on the decision whether or not to build a new office building, a school, a hospital or a prison, or on what its function should or could be. They have had practically no impact on the decision to perform surgery on a critically sick patient or on what surgery to perform. They have had no impact on the decision of the equipment manufacturer concerning which markets to enter and with which products, or on the decision of a major bank to acquire another major bank. For top management tasks, information technology so far has been a producer of data rather than a producer of information—let alone a producer of new and different questions and new and different strategies.

The people in Management Information Systems (MIS) and in Information Technology (IT) tend to blame this failure on what they call the "reactionary" executives of the "old school." It is the wrong explanation. Top executives have not used the new technology because it has not provided the information they need for *their own tasks*. The data available in business enterprise are, for instance, still largely based on the early-19th-century theorem that lower costs differentiate businesses and make them compete successfully. MIS has taken the data based on this theorem and computerized them. They are the data of the traditional accounting system. Accounting was originally created, at least five hundred years ago, to provide the data a company needed for the preservation of its assets and for their distribution if the venture were liquidated. And the one major addition to accounting since the 15th century—cost accounting, a child of the 1920s—aimed only at bringing the accounting system up to 19th-century economics, namely, to provide information about, and control of, costs. (So does, by the way, the now-so-popular revision of cost accounting: total quality management.)

But, as we began to realize around the time of World War II, neither preservation of assets nor cost control is a top management task. They are OPERATIONAL TASKS. A serious cost disadvantage may indeed destroy a business. But business *success* is based on something totally different, the *creation of value and wealth*. This requires risk-taking decisions: on the theory of the business, on business strategy, on abandoning the old and innovating the new, on the balance between immediate profitability and market share. It requires strategic decisions based on the *New Certainties* discussed in Chapter Two. These decisions are the true top management tasks. It was this recognition that underlay, after World War II, the emergence of management as a discipline, separate and distinct from what was then called business economics and is now called microeconomics. But for none of these top management tasks does the traditional accounting system provide information. Indeed, none of these tasks is even compatible with the assumptions of the traditional accounting model. The new information technology, based on the computer, had no choice but to depend on the accounting system's data. No others were available. It collected these data, systematized them, manipulated them, analyzed them and presented them. On this rested, in large measure, the tremendous impact the new technology had on what cost accounting data were designed for: operations. But it also explains information technology's near-zero impact on the management of business itself.

Top management's frustration with the data that information technology has so far provided has triggered the new, the next, Information Revolution. Information technologists, especially chief information officers in businesses, soon realized that the accounting data are not what their associates need—which largely explains why MIS and IT people tend to be contemptuous of accounting and accountants. But they did not, as a rule, realize that what was needed was not more data, more technology, more speed. What was needed was to define information; what was needed was *new concepts*. And in one enterprise after another, top management people during the last few years have begun to ask, "What information concepts do we need for our tasks?" And they have now begun to demand them of their traditional information providers, the accounting people.

The new accounting that is evolving as a result of these questions will be discussed in a later section of this chapter ("The Information Enterprises Need"). And so is the one new area—and

the most important one—in which we do not as yet have systematic and organized methods for obtaining information: information on the OUTSIDE of the enterprise. These new methods are
very different in their assumptions and their origins. Each was
developed independently and by different people. But they all
have two things in common. They aim at providing information
rather than data. And they are designed for top management and
to provide information for top management tasks and top management decisions.

The new Information Revolution began in business and
has gone farthest in it. But it is about to revolutionize
education and health care. Again, the changes in concepts
will in the end be at least as important as the changes in
tools and technology. It is generally accepted now that
education technology is due for profound changes and
that with them will come profound changes in structure.
Long-distance learning, for instance, may well make obsolete within twenty-five years that uniquely American institution, the freestanding undergraduate college. It is
becoming clearer every day that these technical changes
will—indeed must—lead to redefining what is meant by
education. One probable consequence: The center of gravity in higher education (i.e., postsecondary teaching and
learning) may shift to the continuing professional education of adults during their entire working lives. This, in
turn, is likely to move learning off campus and into a lot
of new places: the home, the car or the commuter train,
the workplace, the church basement or the school audito-
rium where small groups can meet after hours.

In health care a similar conceptual shift is likely to
lead from health care being defined as the fight against
disease to being defined as the maintenance of physical
and mental functioning. The fight against disease
remains an important part of medical care, of course, but
as what a logician would call a subset of it. Neither of the
traditional health care providers, the hospital and the

general practice physician, may survive this change, and certainly not in their present form and function.

In education and health care, the emphasis thus will also shift from the "T" in IT to the "I," as it is shifting in business.

The Lessons of History

The current Information Revolution is actually the fourth Information Revolution in human history. The first one was the invention of writing five thousand to six thousand years ago in Mesopotamia; then—independently but several thousand years later—in China; and some fifteen hundred years later still, by the Maya in Central America. The second Information Revolution was brought on by the invention of the written book, first in China, perhaps as early as 1300 B.C., and then, independently, eight hundred years later, in Greece, when Peisistratos, the tyrant of Athens, had Homer's epics—only recited until then—copied into books. The third Information Revolution was set off by Gutenberg's invention of the printing press and of movable type between 1450 and 1455, and by the contemporaneous invention of engraving. We have almost no documents on the first two of these revolutions, though we know that the impact of the written book was enormous in Greece and Rome as well as in China. In fact, China's entire civilization and system of government still rest on it. But on the third Information Revolution, printing and engraving, we have abundant material. Is there anything we can learn today from what happened five hundred years ago?

The first thing to learn is a little humility.
Everybody today believes that the present Information Revolution is unprecedented in reducing the cost of, and in the spreading of, information—whether measured by the cost of a "byte" or by computer ownership—and in the speed and sweep of its impact. These beliefs are simply nonsense.
At the time Gutenberg introduced the press, there was a sub-

stantial information industry in Europe. It was probably Europe's biggest employer. It consisted of hundreds of monasteries, many of which housed large numbers of highly skilled monks. Each monk labored from dawn to dusk, six days a week, copying books by hand. An industrious, well-trained monk could do four pages a day, or twenty-five pages during a six-day week, for an annual output of twelve hundred to thirteen hundred handwritten pages.

Fifty years later, by 1500, the monks had become unemployed. These monks (some estimates go well above ten thousand for all of Europe) had been replaced by a very small number of lay craftsmen, the new "printers," totaling perhaps one thousand, but spread over all of Europe (though only beginning to establish themselves in Scandinavia). To produce a printed book required coordinated teamwork by up to twenty such craftsmen, beginning with one highly skilled cutter of type, to a much larger number, maybe ten or more, of much less skilled bookbinders. Such a team produced each year about twenty-five titles, with an average of two hundred pages per title, or five thousand pages ready to be printed. By 1505, print runs of one thousand copies became possible. This meant that a printing team could produce annually at least 5 *million* printed pages, bound into 25,000 books ready to be sold—or 250,000 pages per team member as against the twelve hundred or thirteen hundred the individual monk had produced only fifty years earlier.

Prices fell dramatically. As late as the mid-1400s—just before Gutenberg's invention—books were such a luxury that only the wealthy and educated could afford them. But when Martin Luther's German Bible came out in 1522 (a book of well over one thousand pages), its price was so low that even the poorest peasant family could buy one.

The cost and price reductions of the third Information Revolution were at least as great as those of the present, the fourth Information Revolution. And so were the speed and the extent of its spread.

This has been just as true of every other major technological revolution. Though cotton was by far the most desirable of all textile fibers—it is easily washable and can be worked up into an infinite variety of different cloths—it required a time- and labor-expensive process. It took twelve to fourteen man-*days* to produce a pound of cotton yarn by hand, as against one to two man-days for wool, two to five for linen and six for silk. Between 1764, when machine tools to work cotton were first introduced—triggering the Industrial Revolution—and 1784, the time needed to produce a pound of cotton yarn fell to a few hours. (This interval, incidentally, is exactly the same as that between the ENIAC and IBM's 360.) The price dropped by 70 percent and production rose twenty-five-fold. Yet this was still before Eli Whitney's cotton gin (1793), which produced a further fall in the price of cotton yarn of 90 percent-plus and ultimately to about a thousandth of what it had been before the Industrial Revolution of fifty or sixty years earlier.

Just as important as the reduction in costs and the speed of the new printing technology was its impact on what information meant. The first printed books, beginning with Gutenberg's Bible, were in Latin and still had the same topics as the books that the monks had earlier written out by hand: religious and philosophical treatises and whatever texts had survived from Latin antiquity. But only twenty years after Gutenberg's invention, books by contemporary authors began to emerge, though they still appeared in Latin. Another ten years and books were printed not only in Greek and Hebrew but also, increasingly, in the vernacular (first in English, then in the other European tongues). And in 1476, only twenty years after Gutenberg, the English printer William Caxton (1422–1491) published a book on so worldly a subject as chess. By 1500, popular literature no longer meant verse—epics, especially—that lent themselves to oral transmission, but prose, that is, the printed book.

In no time at all, the printing revolution also changed institutions, including the educational system. In the decades that followed, university after university was founded throughout Europe, but unlike the earlier ones, they weren't designed for the clergy or for the study of theology. They were built around disciplines for the laity: law, medicine, mathematics, natural philosophy (science). And eventually—though it took two hundred years—the printed book created universal education and the present school.

Printing's greatest impact, however, was on the core of pre-Gutenberg Europe: the church. Printing made the Protestant Reformation possible. Its predecessors, the reformations of John Wycliffe in England (1330–1384) and of Jan Hus in Bohemia (1372–1415), had met with an equally enthusiastic popular response. But those revolts could not travel farther or faster than the spoken word and could thus be localized and suppressed. This was not the case when Luther, on October 31, 1517, nailed his ninety-five theses on a church door in an obscure German town. He had intended only to initiate a traditional theological debate within the church. But without Luther's consent (and probably without his knowledge), the theses were immediately printed and distributed gratis all over Germany, and then all over Europe. These printed leaflets ignited the religious firestorm that turned into the Reformation.

Would there have been an age of discovery, beginning in the second half of the 15th century, without the printing press? Printing publicized every single advance the Portuguese seafarers made along the west coast of Africa in their search for a sea route to the Indies. Printing provided Columbus with the first (though totally wrong) maps of the fabled lands beyond the western horizon, such as Marco Polo's China and the legendary Japan. Printing made it possible to record the results of every single voyage immediately and to create new, more reliable maps.

Noneconomic changes cannot be quantified. But the impact on society, education, culture—let alone on religion—of the printing revolution was easily as great and surely as fast as the impact of the present Information Revolution, if not faster.

History's Lesson for the Technologists

The last Information Revolution, the printed book, may also have a lesson for today's information technologists, the IT and MIS people and the CIOs: They will not disappear. But they may be about to become "Supporting Cast" rather than the "Superstars" they have been the last forty years.

The printing revolution immediately created a new class of information technologists, just as the most recent Information Revolution has created any number of information businesses, MIS and IT specialists, software designers and chief information officers. The IT people of the printing revolution were the early printers. Nonexistent—and indeed not even imaginable—in 1455, they had become stars twenty-five years later. These virtuosi of the printing press were known and revered all over Europe, just as the names of the leading computer and software firms are recognized and admired worldwide today. Printers were courted by kings, princes, the Pope and rich merchant cities and were showered with money and honors.

> The first of these tycoons was the famous Venetian printer Aldus Manutius (1449–1515). He realized that the new printing press could make a large number of impressions from the same plate—a thousand by the year 1505. He created the low-cost, mass-produced book. Aldus Manutius created the printing industry: He was the first to extend printing to languages other than Latin and also the first to do books by contemporary authors. Altogether his press turned out well over one thousand titles.
>
> The last of these great printing technologists, and also the last of the printing princes, was Christophe Plantin (1520–1589) of Antwerp. Starting as a humble apprentice binder, he built Europe's biggest and most famous printing firm. By marrying the two new technologies, printing and engraving, he created the illustrated book. He became Antwerp's leading patrician (Antwerp was then one of the richest cities in Europe, if not the world), and he became so wealthy that he was able to build himself a magnificent

palace, still preserved today as a printing museum. But Plantin and his printing house began to decline well before his death and soon faded into insignificance.

By 1580 or so, the printers, with their focus on technology, had become ordinary craftsmen, respectable tradesmen to be sure, but definitely no longer of the upper class. And they had also ceased both to be more profitable than other trades and to attract investment capital. Their place was soon taken by what we now call publishers (though the term wasn't coined until much later), people and firms whose focus was no longer on the "T" in IT but on the "I."

This shift got under way the moment the new technology began to have an impact on the MEANING of information, and with it, on the meaning and function of the 15th century's key institutions such as the church and the universities. It thus began at the same juncture at which we now find ourselves in the present Information Revolution. Is this where Information *Technology* and Information *Technologists* are now?

The New Print Revolution

There is actually no reason to believe that the new Information Revolution has to be "high-tech" at all. For we did have a real "Information Revolution" these last fifty years, from 1950 on. But it is not based on computers and electronics. The real boom— and it has been a veritable boom—has been in that old "no-tech" medium, PRINT.

In 1950 when television first swept the country, it was widely believed that it would be the end of the printed book. U.S. population since has grown by two-thirds. The number of college and university students—the most concentrated group of users and buyers of books—has increased five-fold. But the number of printed books published and bought in the U.S. has grown at least fifteen-fold, and probably closer to twenty-fold.

It is generally believed that the leading "high-tech" companies—IBM in the sixties and seventies, Microsoft since 1980—have been the fastest-growing businesses in the post–World War II period. But the world's two leading *print* companies have grown at least as fast. One is the German-based Bertelsmann Group. A small publisher of Protestant prayer books before Hitler, Bertelsmann was suppressed by the Nazis. It was revived after World War II by the founder's grandson, Reinhard Mohn. Still privately held, Bertelsmann publishes no sales or profit figures. But it is now the world's number one publisher and distributor of printed materials (other than daily papers) in most countries of the world (except in China and Russia), through its ownership of publishing firms (e.g., of Random House in the United States), of book clubs and of magazines (e.g., of France's leading business magazine *Capital*). Equally fast has been the growth of the empire of the Australian-born Rupert Murdoch. Starting as publisher of two small provincial Australian daily papers, Murdoch now owns newspapers throughout the English-speaking world, leading English-language book publishers and magazines—but also a large company in another precomputer "information medium," the movies.

Even faster than the growth of these BOOK publishers has been the growth of another PRINT medium: the "specialty mass magazine." A good many of the huge-circulation "general magazines" that dominated 1920s and 1930s America, *Life*, for instance, or *The Saturday Evening Post*, have disappeared. They did indeed fall victim to television. But there are in the United States now several THOUSAND—one estimate is more than THREE THOUSAND—specialty mass magazines, each with a circulation between fifty thousand and a million, and most highly profitable.

The most visible examples are magazines that cover business or the economy. The three leading American magazines of this type, *Business Week* (a weekly), *Fortune* (a biweekly), and *Forbes* (a monthly), each have a circulation approaching 1 million. Before World War II the London-based *Economist*—the world's only magazine that systematically reports every week on economics, politics and business all the world over—was practically unknown outside the UK, and even there its circulation was quite small, well below one hundred thousand copies. Now its U.S. circulation alone exceeds three hundred thousand copies a week.

But there are similar specialty mass-circulation magazines in every field and for every interest—in health care and in running symphony orchestras, in psychology and in foreign affairs, in architecture and home maintenance and computers and, above all, for every single profession, every single trade, every single industry. One of the most successful—and one of the earliest ones—is *Scientific American,* a U.S. monthly founded (or rather refounded) in the late 1940s, in which distinguished scientists explain their own specialized scientific area to the "scientific laity," that is, to scientists in other specialties.

And what explains the success of the PRINT media?

College students probably account for the largest single share of the growth of printed books in the United States. It is growth in college texts and in books assigned by college teachers. But the second largest group are books that did not exist before the 1950s, at least not in any quantity. There is no English word for them. But the German publisher who first saw their potential and first founded a publishing house expressly to publish such books, the late E. B. von Wehrenalp (who founded Econ Verlag in Duesseldorf—still my German publisher), called it the *Sachbuch*—a book written by an expert for nonexperts. And when asked to explain the *Sachbuch* Wehrenalp said: "It has to be enjoyable reading. It has to be educational. But its purpose is neither entertainment nor education. Its purpose is INFORMATION."

This is just as true of the specialty mass magazines—whether written for the layman who wants to know about medicine or for the plumber who wants to know what goes on in the plumbing business. THEY INFORM. And above all, they inform about the OUTSIDE. The specialty mass magazine tells the reader in a profession, a trade, an industry what goes on outside his or her own business, shop or office—about the competition, about new products and new technology, about developments in other countries and above all, about people in the profession, the trade, the industry (and gossip has always had the highest information—or misinformation—quotient of all communication).

And now the printed media are taking over the electronic channels. The fastest-growing book seller since Aldus Manutius five hundred years ago has been Amazon.com, which sells printed books over the Internet. In a few very short years it may have become the Internet's largest retail merchant. And Bertelsmann, in the fall of 1998, bought a controlling 50 percent in Barnes & Noble, Amazon's main competitor. More and more of the specialty mass magazines now publish an "on-line" edition—delivered over the Internet to be printed out by the subscriber. Instead of IT *replacing* print, print is taking over the electronic technology as a distribution channel for PRINTED INFORMATION.

The new distribution channel will surely change the printed book. New distribution channels always do change what they distribute. But however delivered or stored, it will remain a *printed* product. And it will still provide *information*.

The market for information exists, in other words. And, though still disorganized, so does the supply. In the next few years—surely not much more than a decade or two—the two will converge. And that will be the REAL NEW INFORMATION REVOLUTION—led not by IT people, but by accountants and publishers. And then both enterprises and individuals will have to learn what information they need and how to get it. THEY WILL HAVE TO LEARN TO ORGANIZE INFORMATION AS THEIR KEY RESOURCE.

II
The Information Enterprises Need

We are just beginning to understand how to use information as a tool. But we already can outline the major parts of the information system enterprises need. In turn, we can begin to understand the concepts likely to underlie the enterprise that executives will have to manage tomorrow.

From Cost Accounting to Result Control

We may have gone furthest in redesigning both enterprise and information in the most traditional of our information systems: accounting. In fact, many businesses have already shifted from traditional cost accounting to *activity-based costing*. It was first developed for manufacturing where it is now in wide use. But it is rapidly spreading to service businesses and even to nonbusinesses, for example, universities. Activity-based costing represents both a different concept of the business process and different ways of measuring.

> Traditional cost accounting, first developed by General Motors seventy years ago, postulates that total manufacturing cost is the sum of the costs of individual operations. Yet the cost that matters for competitiveness and profitability is the cost of the total process, and that is what the new *activity-based costing* records and makes manageable. Its basic premise is that business is an integrated process that starts when supplies, materials and parts arrive at the plant's loading dock and continues even after the finished product reaches the end-user. Service is still a cost of the product, and so is installation, even if the customer pays.

Traditional cost accounting measures what it costs to *do* something, for example, to cut a screw thread. Activity-based costing also records the cost of *not doing*, such as the cost of machine downtime, the cost of waiting for a needed part or tool, the cost of inventory waiting to be shipped and the cost of reworking or scrapping a defective part. The *costs of not doing*, which traditional cost accounting cannot and does not record, often equal and sometimes even exceed the cost of doing, Activity-based costing therefore gives not only much better cost control; increasingly, it gives *result control*.

Traditional cost accounting assumes that a certain operation—for example, heat treating—has to be done and that it has to be done where it is being done now. Activity-based costing asks,

"Does it have to be done? If so, where is it best done?" Activity-based costing integrates what were once several procedures—value analysis, process analysis, quality management and costing—into one analysis.

Using that approach, activity-based costing can substantially lower manufacturing costs—in some instances by a full third. Its greatest impact, however, is likely to be in *services*. In most manufacturing companies, cost accounting is inadequate. But service industries—banks, retail stores, hospitals, schools, newspapers and radio and television stations—have practically no cost information at all. Activity-based costing shows why traditional cost accounting has not worked for service companies. It is not because the techniques are wrong. It is because traditional cost accounting makes the wrong assumptions. Service companies cannot start with the cost of individual operations, as manufacturing companies have done with traditional cost accounting. They must start with the assumption that there is only *one* cost: that of the total system. And it is a fixed cost over any given time period. The famous distinction between fixed and variable costs, on which traditional cost accounting is based, does not make sense in services. Neither does another basic assumption of traditional cost accounting: that capital can be substituted for labor. In fact, in knowledge-based work especially, additional capital investment is likely to require more rather than less labor. A hospital that buys a new diagnostic tool will not lay off anybody as a result. But it will have to add four or five people to run the new equipment. Other knowledge-based organizations have had to learn the same lesson. But that all costs are fixed over a given time period and that resources cannot be substituted for each other are precisely the assumptions with which activity-based costing starts. By applying them to services, we are beginning for the first time to get cost information and control.

> Banks, for instance, have been trying for several decades to apply conventional cost-accounting techniques to their business—that is, to figure the costs of individual operations and services—with almost negligible results. Now they are beginning to ask, "Which one *activity* is at the cen-

ter of costs and of results?" One answer: the customer. The cost per customer in any major area of banking is a fixed cost. Thus it is the *yield* per customer—both the volume of services a customer uses and the mix of those services—that determines costs and profitability. Retail discounters, especially those in Western Europe, have known that for some time. They assume that once shelf space is installed, its cost is fixed, and management consists of maximizing the yield on the space over a given time span. This focus on result control has enabled these discounters to increase profitability despite their low prices and low margins.

In some areas, such as research labs, where productivity is difficult to measure, we may always have to rely on assessment and judgment rather than on costing. But for most knowledge-based and service work, we should, within ten years, have developed reliable tools to measure and manage costs and to relate those costs to results.

Thinking more clearly about costing in services should yield new insights into the costs of getting and keeping customers in businesses of all kinds.

If GM, Ford and Chrysler in the United States had used activity-based costing, for example, they would have realized early on the utter futility of their competitive "blitzes" of the past twenty years, which offered new-car buyers spectacular discounts and hefty cash rewards. Those promotions actually cost the Big Three automakers enormous amounts of money and, worse, enormous numbers of customers. In fact, every one resulted in a nasty drop in market standing. But neither the costs of the special deals nor their negative yields appeared in the companies' conventional cost-accounting figures, so management never saw the damage.

Because the Japanese used a form of activity-based costing—though a fairly primitive one—Toyota, Nissan and Honda knew better than to compete with the U.S. automakers through discount blitzes, and thus maintained both their market share and their profits.

From Legal Fiction to Economic Reality

Knowing the cost of operations, however, is not enough. To compete successfully in an increasingly competitive global market, a company has to know the costs of its *entire economic chain* and has to work with other members of the chain to manage costs and maximize yield. Companies are therefore beginning to shift from costing only what goes on inside their own organizations to costing the entire economic process, in which even the biggest company is just one link.

The legal entity, the company, is a reality for shareholders, for creditors, for employees, and for tax collectors. But *economically*, it is fiction.

> Thirty years ago the Coca-Cola Company was a franchiser all over the world. Independent bottlers manufactured the product. Now the company owns most of its bottling operations in the United States. But Coke drinkers—even those few who know that fact—could not care less.

What matters in the marketplace is the economic reality, the costs of the entire process, regardless of who owns what.

Again and again in business history, an unknown company has come from nowhere and in a few short years has overtaken the established leaders without apparently even breathing hard. The explanation always given is superior strategy, superior technology, superior marketing, or lean manufacturing. But in every single case, the newcomer also enjoys a tremendous cost advantage, usually about 30 percent. The reason is always the same: the new company knows and manages the costs of the entire economic chain rather than its costs alone.

> Toyota is perhaps the best-publicized example of a company that knows and manages the costs of its suppliers and distributors; they are all, of course, members of its Keiretsu. Through that network, Toyota manages the total cost of making, distributing and servicing its cars as one cost stream, putting work where it costs the least and yields the most. (On the history of the Keiretsu see Chapter One.)

Economists have known the importance of costing the entire economic chain since Alfred Marshall wrote about it in the late 1890s. But most business people still consider it theoretical abstraction. Increasingly, however, managing the economic cost chain will become a necessity. Indeed, executives need to organize and manage not only the cost chain but also everything else—especially corporate strategy and product planning—as one economic whole, regardless of the legal boundaries of individual companies.

A powerful force driving companies toward economic chain costing will be the shift from *cost-led pricing* to *price-led costing*. Traditionally, Western companies have started with costs, put a desired profit margin on top, and arrived at a price. They practiced cost-led pricing. Sears and Marks & Spencer long ago switched to price-led costing, in which the price the customer is willing to pay determines allowable costs, beginning with the design stage. Until recently, those companies were the exceptions. Now price-led costing is becoming the rule.

The same ideas apply to *outsourcing, alliances* and *joint ventures*—indeed, to any structure that is built on partnership rather than control. And such entities, rather than the traditional model of a parent company with wholly owned subsidiaries, are increasingly becoming the models for growth, especially in the global economy. (On this see Chapter One.)

For many businesses it will be painful to switch to economic-chain costing. Doing so requires uniform or at least compatible accounting systems of all companies along the entire chain. Yet each one does its accounting in its own way, and each is convinced that its system is the only possible one. Moreover, economic-chain costing requires information sharing across companies; yet even within the same company, people tend to resist information sharing.

Whatever the obstacles, economic-chain costing is going to be done. Otherwise, even the most efficient company will suffer from an increasing cost disadvantage.

Information for Wealth Creation

Enterprises are paid to create wealth, not to control costs. But that obvious fact is not reflected in traditional measurements. First-year accounting students are taught that the balance sheet portrays the liquidation value of the enterprise and provides creditors with worst-case information. But enterprises are not normally run to be liquidated. They have to be managed as going concerns, that is, for *wealth creation*.

To do that requires four sets of diagnostic tools: foundation information, productivity information, competence information, and resource allocation information. Together they constitute the executive's tool kit for managing the current business.

Foundation Information

The oldest and most widely used set of diagnostic management tools are cash-flow and liquidity projections and such standard measurements as the ratio between dealers' inventories and sales of new cars, the earnings coverage for interest payments on a bond issue, and the ratios between receivables outstanding more than six months, total receivables, and sales. Those may be likened to the measurements a doctor takes at a routine physical: weight, pulse, temperature, blood pressure and urinalysis. If those readings are normal, they do not tell us much. If they are abnormal, they indicate a problem that needs to be identified and treated. Those measurements might be called *foundation information*.

Productivity Information

The second set of tools for business diagnosis deals with the *productivity of key resources*. The oldest of them—of World War II vintage—measures the productivity of manual labor. Now we are slowly developing measurements though still quite primitive ones, for the productivity of knowledge-based and service work (see Chapter Five). However, measuring only the productivity of workers, whether blue- or white-collar, no longer gives us adequate information about productivity. We need data on *total-factor productivity*.

That explains the growing popularity of Economic Value-Added Analysis (EVA). It is based on something we have known for a long time: What we generally call profits, the money left to service equity, is not profit at all and may be mostly a genuine cost. Until a business returns a profit that is greater than its cost of capital, it operates at a loss. Never mind that it pays taxes as if it had a genuine profit. The enterprise still returns less to the economy than it uses up in resources. It does not cover its full costs unless the reported profit exceeds the cost of capital. Until then, it does not create wealth; it destroys it. By that measurement, incidentally, few U.S. businesses have been profitable since World War II.

> By measuring the value added over *all* costs, including the cost of capital, EVA measures, in effect, the productivity of *all* factors of production. It does not, by itself, tell us why a certain product or a certain service does not add value or what to do about it. But it shows us what we need to find out and that we need to take action. EVA should also be used to find out what works. It does show which products, services, operations or activities have unusually high productivity and add unusually high value. Then we should ask ourselves, "What can we learn from these successes?"

The most recent of the tools used to obtain productivity information is *benchmarking*—comparing one's performance with the best performance in the industry or, better yet, with the best anywhere in the world. Benchmarking assumes correctly that what one organization does, any other organization can do as well. It assumes correctly that any business has to be globally competitive (see Chapter Two). It assumes, also correctly, that being at least as good as the leader is a prerequisite to being competitive. Together, EVA and benchmarking provide the diagnostic tools to measure total-factor productivity and to manage it.

Competence Information

A third set of tools deals with competences. Leadership rests on being able to do something others cannot do at all or find difficult to do even poorly. It rests on *core competencies* that meld market or customer value with a special ability of the producer or supplier.

> Some examples: the ability of the Japanese to miniaturize electronic components, which is based on their three-hundred-year-old artistic tradition of putting landscape paintings on a tiny lacquered box, called an *inro*, and of carving a whole zoo of animals on the even tinier button, called a *netsuke*, that holds the box on the wearer's belt; or the almost unique ability GM has had for eighty years to make successful acquisitions; or Marks & Spencer's also unique ability to design packaged and ready-to-eat gourmet meals for middle-class purses. But how does one identify both the core competencies one has already and those the business needs to take and maintain a leadership position? How does one find out whether one's core competence is improving or weakening? Or whether it is still the right core competence and what changes it might need?

> So far the discussion of core competencies has been largely anecdotal. But a number of highly specialized, midsized companies—a Swedish pharmaceutical producer and a U.S. producer of specialty tools, to name two—are developing the methodology to measure and manage core competencies.

> The first step is to keep careful track of one's own and one's competitors' performance, looking especially for unexpected successes and for unexpected poor performance in areas where one should have done well. The successes demonstrate what the market values and will pay for. They indicate where the business enjoys a leadership advantage. The nonsuccesses should be viewed as the first

indication either that the market is changing or that the company's competencies are weakening.

This analysis allows for the early recognition of opportunities.

By carefully tracking unexpected successes, a U.S. tool-maker found, for example, that small Japanese machine shops were buying its high-tech, high-priced tools, even though it had not designed the tools with them in mind or ever offered these tools to them. That allowed the company to recognize a new core competence: its products were easy to maintain and to repair despite their technical complexity. When that insight was applied to designing products, the company gained leadership in the small-plant and machine-shop markets in the United States and Western Europe, huge markets where it had done practically no business before.

Core competencies are different for every organization; they are, so to speak, part of an organization's personality. But every organization—not just businesses—needs one core competence: *innovation*. And every organization needs a way to record and appraise its *innovative performance*. In organizations already doing that—among them several topflight pharmaceutical manufacturers—the starting point is not the company's own performance. It is a careful record of the innovations in the entire field during a given period. Which of them were truly successful? How many of them were ours? Is our performance commensurate with our objectives? With the direction of the market? With our market standing? With our research spending? Are our successful innovations in the areas of greatest growth and opportunity? How many of the truly important innovation opportunities did we miss? Why? Because we did not see them? Or because we saw them but dismissed them? Or because we botched them? And how well do we do in converting an innovation into a commercial product? A good deal of that, admittedly, is assessment rather than measurement. It raises rather than answers questions, but it raises the right questions.

Resource Allocation Information

The last area in which diagnostic information is needed to manage the current business for wealth creation is the *allocation of scarce resources*: capital and performing people. Those two convert into action all the information that a management has about its business. They determine whether the enterprise will do well or poorly.

GM developed the first systematic capital-appropriations process about seventy years ago. Today practically every business has a capital-appropriations process, but few use it correctly. Companies typically measure their proposed capital appropriations by only one or two of the following yardsticks: return on investment, payback period, cash flow, or discounted present value. But we have known for a long time—since the early 1930s—that none of those is *the* right method. To understand a proposed investment, a company needs *to look to all four.* Sixty years ago that would have required endless number-crunching. Now a laptop computer can provide the data within a few minutes. We also have known for sixty years that managers should never look at just one proposed capital appropriation in isolation but should instead choose the projects that show the best ratio between opportunity and risks. That requires a capital-appropriations *budget* to display the choices—again, something far too many businesses do not do.

Most serious, however, is that most capital-appropriations processes do not even ask for two vital pieces of information:

- What will happen if the proposed investment fails to produce the promised results, as do three out of every five? Would it seriously hurt the company, or would it be just a fleabite?

- If the investment is successful—and especially if it is more successful than we expect—what will it commit us to?

In addition, a capital-appropriations request requires specific deadlines: When should we expect what results? Then the results—successes, near successes, near failures, and failures— need to be reported and analyzed. There is no better way to improve an organization's performance than to measure the results of capital spending against the promises and expectations that led to its authorization. How much better off would the United States be today had such feedback on government programs been standard practice for the past fifty years?

Capital, however, is only one key resource of the organization, and it is by no means the scarcest one. The scarcest resources in any organization are *performing people*.

> Since World War II, the U.S. military—and so far no one else—has learned to test its placement decisions. It now thinks through what it expects of senior officers before it puts them into key commands. It then appraises their performance against those expectations. And it constantly appraises its own process for selecting senior commanders against the successes and failures of its appointments.

In business—but in universities, hospitals and government agencies as well—placement with specific expectations as to what the appointee should achieve and systematic appraisal of the outcome are virtually unknown. In the effort to create wealth, managers need to allocate human resources as purposefully and as thoughtfully as they do capital. And the outcomes of those decisions ought to be recorded and studied as carefully.

Where the Results Are

Those four kinds of information tell us only about the current business. They inform and direct *tactics*. For *strategy*, we need organized information about the environment. Strategy has to be based on information about markets, customers and noncustomers; about technology in one's own industry and others; about worldwide finance, and about the changing world economy. For that is where the results are. Inside an organization there are only cost centers. The only profit center is a customer whose check has not bounced.

Major changes always start outside an organization. A retailer may know a great deal about the people who shop at its stores. But no matter how successful, no retailer ever has more than a small fraction of the market as its customers; the great majority are noncustomers. It is always with noncustomers that basic changes begin and become significant. At least half the important new technologies that have transformed an industry in the past fifty years came from outside the industry itself. Commercial paper, which has revolutionized finance in the United States, did not originate with the banks. Molecular biology and genetic engineering were not developed by the pharmaceutical industry. Though the great majority of businesses will continue to operate only locally or regionally, they all face, at least potentially, global competition from places they have never even heard of before.

Not all of the needed information about the outside is available, to be sure, despite the specialty mass magazines. There is no information—not even unreliable information—on economic conditions in most of China, for instance, or on legal conditions in the successor states to the Soviet empire. But even where information is readily available, many businesses are oblivious to it. Many U.S. companies went into Europe in the 1960s without even asking about labor legislation. European companies have been just as blind and ill-informed in their ventures into the United States. A major cause of the Japanese real estate investment debacle in California during the 1990s was the failure to find out elementary facts about zoning and taxes.

A serious cause of business failure is the common assumption that conditions—taxes, social legislation, market preferences, distribution channels, intellectual property rights and many others—*must* be what we think they are or at least what we think they *should* be.

An adequate information system has to include information that makes executives question that assumption. It must lead them to ask the right questions, not just feed them the information they expect. That presupposes first that executives know what information they need. It demands further that they obtain that information on a regular basis. It finally requires that they systematically integrate the information into their decision making.

These are beginnings. These are first attempts to organize "Business Intelligence," that is, information about actual and potential competitors worldwide. A few multinationals—Unilever, Coca-Cola, Nestlé, some Japanese trading companies, and a few big construction companies—have been working hard on building systems to gather and organize outside information. But in general, the majority of enterprises have yet to start the job. It is fast becoming the major information challenge for all enterprises.

III
The Information Executives Need for Their Work

A great deal of the new technology has been *data processing* equipment for the individual. But as far as *information* goes, the attention has been mainly on information for the enterprise—as it has been so far in this chapter. But information for executives—and indeed, for all knowledge workers—for their own work may be a great deal more important. For the knowledge worker in general, and especially for executives, information is their key resource. Information increasingly creates the link to their fellow workers and to the organization, and their "network." It is information, in other words, that enables knowledge workers to do their job.

By now it is clear that no one can provide the information that knowledge workers and especially executives need, except knowledge workers and executives themselves. But few executives so far have made much of an effort to decide what they need, and even less, how to organize it. They have tended to rely on the producers of data—IT people and accountants—to make these decisions for them. But the *producers* of data cannot possibly know what data the *users* need so that they become information. Only individual knowledge workers, and especially individual executives, can convert data into information. And only individual knowledge workers, and especially individual executives, can decide how to organize their information so that it becomes their key to effective action.

To produce the information executives need for their work, they have to begin with two questions:

"What information do I owe to the people with whom I work and on whom I depend? In what form? And in what time frame?"

"What information do I need myself? From whom? In what form? And in what time frame?"

These two questions are closely connected. But they are different. *What I owe* comes first because it establishes *communications*. And unless that has been established, there will be no information flow back to the executive.

We have known this since Chester I. Barnard (1886–1961) published his pioneering book *The Functions of the Executive*, in 1938, over sixty years ago. Yet, while Barnard's book is universally praised, it has had little practical impact. Communication for Barnard was vague and general. It was human relationships, and personal. However, what makes communications effective at the workplace is that they are focused on something *outside* the person. They have to be focused on a common task and on a common challenge. They have to be focused on the *work*.

And by asking: "To whom do I owe information, so that *they* can do their work?" communications are being focused on the common task and the common work. They become effective. The first question therefore (as in any effective relationship), is not: "What do *I* want and need?" It is: "What do *other people* need from me?" and "Who are these other people?" Only then can the question be asked: "What information do I need? From whom? In what form? In what time frame?"

Executives who ask these questions will soon find that little of the information they need comes out of their own company's information system. Some comes out of accounting—though in many cases the accounting data has to be rethought, reformulated, rearranged to apply to the executive's own work. But a good deal of the information executives need for their own work will come, as said already, from the outside and will have to be organized quite separately and distinctly from the inside information system.

The only one who can answer the question: "What do I owe by way of information? To whom? In what form?" is the *other person*. The first step in obtaining the information that executives need for their own work is, therefore, to go to everyone with whom they work, everyone on whom they depend, everyone who needs to know what they themselves are doing, and ask them. But before one asks, one has to be prepared to answer. For the other person will—and should—come back and ask: "And what information do *you* need from me?" Hence, executives need first to think through *both* questions—but then they start out by going to the other people and ask them first to tell them: "What do *I* owe you?"

Both questions, "What do I owe?" and "What do I need?" sound deceptively simple. But everyone who has asked them has soon found out that it takes a lot of thought, a lot of experimentation, a lot of hard work, to answer them. And the answers are not forever. In fact, these questions have to be asked again, every eighteen months or so. They also have to be asked every time there is a real change, for example, a change in the enterprise's theory of the business, in the individual's own job and assignment, or in the jobs and assignments of the other people.

But if individuals ask these questions seriously, they will soon come to understand both what they need and what they owe. And then they can set about organizing both.

Organizing Information

Unless organized, information is still data. To be meaningful it has to be organized. It is, however, not clear at all in what form certain kinds of information are meaningful, and especially in what form of organization they are meaningful for one's own job. And the same information may have to be organized in different ways for different purposes.

> Here is one example. Since Jack Welch took over as CEO in 1981, the General Electric Company (GE) has created more wealth than any other company in the world. One of the main factors in this success was that GE organized the same information about the performance of every one of its business units differently for different purposes. It kept traditional financial and marketing reporting, the way most companies appraise their businesses every year or so. But the same data were also organized for long-range strategy, that is, to show unexpected successes and unexpected failures, but also to show where actual events differed substantially from what was expected. A third way to organize the same data was to focus on the innovative performance of the business—which became a major factor in determining compensation and bonuses of the general manager and of the senior management people of a business unit. Finally, the same data were organized to show how the business unit and its management treated and developed people—which then became a key factor in deciding on the promotion of an executive, and especially of the general manager of a business unit.

No two executives, in my experience, organize the same information the same way. And information has to be organized the way individual executives work. But there are some basic methodologies to organize information.

One is the *Key Event*. Which events—for it is usually more than one—are the "hinges" on which the rest of *my* performance primarily depends? The key event may be technological—the success of a research project. It may have to do with people and their development. It may have to do with establishing a new product or a new service with certain key customers. It may be to obtain new customers. What is a key event is very much the executive's individual decision. It is, however, a decision that needs to be discussed with the people on whom the executive depends. It is perhaps the most important thing anybody in an organization has to get across to the people with whom one works, and especially to one's own superior.

Another key methodological concept comes out of modern *Probability Theory*—it is the concept on which, for instance, Total Quality Management is based. It is the difference between normal fluctuations within the range of normal probability distribution and the exceptional event. As long as fluctuations stay within the normal distribution of probability for a given type of event (e.g., for quality in a manufacturing process), no action is taken. Such fluctuations are data and not information. But the exception, which falls outside the accepted probability distribution, is information. It calls for action.

Another basic methodology for organizing information comes out of the theory of the *Threshold Phenomenon*—the theory that underlies Perception Psychology. It was a German physicist, Gustav Fechner (1801–1887), who first realized that we do not feel a sensation—for example, a pinprick—until it reaches a certain intensity, that is, until it passes a perception threshold. A great many phenomena follow the same law. They are not actually "phenomena." They are data until they reach a certain intensity, and pass the perception threshold.

For many events, both in one's work and in one's personal life, this theory applies and enables one to organize data into information. When we speak of a "recession" in the economy, we speak of a threshold phenomenon—a downturn in sales and profits is a recession when it passes a certain threshold, for example, when it continues beyond a certain length of time. Similarly, a disease becomes an "epidemic" when, in a certain population, it passes and exceeds a certain threshold.

This concept is particularly useful to organize information about *personnel* events. Such events as accidents, turnover, grievances, and so on become significant when they pass a certain threshold. But the same is true of innovative performance in a company—except that there the perception threshold is the point *below* which a drop in innovative performance becomes relevant and calls for action. The threshold concept is altogether one of the most useful concepts to determine when a sequence of events becomes a "trend," and requires attention and probably action, and when events, even though they may look spectacular, are by themselves not particularly meaningful.

Finally, a good many executives have found that the one way of organizing information effectively is simply to organize one's being informed about the *unusual*.

One example is the "manager's letter." The people who work with a manager write a monthly letter to him or her, reporting on anything unusual and unexpected within their own sphere of work and action. Most of these "unusual" things can safely be disregarded. But again, and again, there is an "exceptional" event, one that is outside the normal range of probability distribution. Again and again, there is a concatenation of events—insignificant in each reporter's area, but significant if added together. Again and again, the management letters bring out a pattern to which to pay attention. Again and again, they convey information.

No Surprises

No system designed by knowledge workers, and especially by executives, to give them the information they need for their work will ever be perfect. But, over the years, they steadily improve. And the ultimate test of an information system is that there are *no surprises*. Before events become significant, executives have already adjusted to them, analyzed them, understood them and taken appropriate action.

> One example are the three or four—very few indeed—American financial institutions that, in the late 1990s, were not surprised by the collapse of mainland Asia. They had thought through what "information" means in respect to Asian economies and Asian currencies. They had gradually eliminated all the information they got from within their own subsidiaries and affiliates in these countries—these, they had begun to realize, were just "data." Instead, they had begun to organize their information about such things as the ratio between fixed investment and portfolio investment in these countries, and the ratio between portfolio investment (i.e., short-term borrowing) and the country's balance of payments and with it the amount available to service foreign short-term debt. Long before these ratios turned so unfavorable as to make a panic in mainland Asia inevitable, these executives had realized that it was coming. They realized that they had to decide whether to pull out of these countries for short-term growth, or to stay for very long-term—and very risky—strategies. They had, in other words, realized what economic data are meaningful in respect to emerging countries, had organized them, had analyzed them and had interpreted them. They had turned the data into information—and had decided what action to take long before that action became necessary.

By contrast, the overwhelming majority of American, European and Asian companies doing business on mainland Asia and/or investing in it relied on what their own people in these countries reported to them. This turned out not to be information at all—in fact it turned out to be misinformation. But only those executives who had spent several years asking the question "What information is meaningful in respect to our doing business in Thailand or Indonesia?" were prepared.

And far too often the mere *quantity* of data is taken to mean information—as if the heft of a big-city telephone book were to make it unnecessary to know whom one wants to reach, what his or her name or business is, and why one wants to talk to the person. Executives have to learn two things: to ELIMINATE data that do not pertain to the information they need; and to organize the data, to analyze, to interpret—and then to focus the resulting information on ACTION. For the purpose of information is not knowledge. It is being able to take the right action.

Going Outside

The example of the companies from the developed countries being surprised by the collapse of the emerging economies of mainland Asia underline the importance of obtaining meaningful *outside* information.

For the executive there is, in the end, only one way to get it: that is to *go, personally, on the outside*. No matter how good the reports, no matter how good the economic or financial theory underlying them, nothing beats personal, direct observation, and in a form in which it is truly *outside* observation.

English supermarket chains have again and again tried to establish themselves in neighboring Ireland—with very little success. The leading supermarket chain in Ireland is Super-Quinn, started and run by Fergal Quinn. His secret is not better merchandise or lower prices. His secret is that he and all of his company's executives have to spend two days a week outside their offices. One day is spent actually doing a job in a supermarket, for example, by serving at a checkout counter or as manager for perishable foods. And one day is spent in competitors' stores watching, listening, talking to the competitors' employees and the competitors' customers.

The largest hospital supply company in the United States was built by a chief executive officer who himself spent four weeks a year—two weeks twice a year—taking the place of a salesman on vacation. He demanded that all the company's senior executives do the same. When the regular salesman came back, the customer—for example, the nun who purchases supplies for the Catholic hospital—always said, "What dumb cluck took your place? He always asked why I buy things from other suppliers rather than from you. He never was particularly interested in getting an order for what you sell." But this was precisely the point of the exercise.

And it is a very old observation that few things improve the performance of a physician as much as being a hospital patient for two weeks.

Market research, focus groups and the like are highly valued, and rightfully so. But still, they always focus on the company's products. They never focus on what the customer buys and is interested in. Only by being a customer oneself, a salesman oneself, a patient oneself, can one get true information about the outside. And even that information is of course still limited to one's customers and one's noncustomers. What other information about the outside do executives need, however, to do their work? And how can they get it?

This is one reason, by the way, why being a volunteer in a nonprofit agency—as discussed in Chapter Six—is important not only for preparing oneself for the second half of one's life. It is equally important as a way to get outside information—which is information on how other people, with other jobs, other backgrounds, other knowledges, other values and other points of view see the world, act and react, and make their decisions. For this reason also, the continuing education of already successful adults will be increasingly important. For in that university course, the forty-five-year-old, successful knowledge worker—business executive, lawyer, university president, minister of a church and so on—is forced to work with people of different backgrounds, and different values. It is one way not only to update one's knowledge but to obtain what executives need: information about the outside.

In the long run, information about the outside may be the most important information executives need to do their work. At the same time, it is the one that still has to be organized. This information is not only the foundation for right action. It is equally the foundation for the challenges discussed in the next two chapters: the challenge of Knowledge-Worker Productivity and the challenge of Managing Oneself. Both rely heavily on the executives knowing what information they need for their work and what information they owe to others, and on systematically developing the methods that turn the chaos of data in the universe into organized and focused information for the executive's own work and job.

5

Knowledge-Worker Productivity

Introduction

The most important, and indeed the truly unique, contribution of management in the 20th century was the fifty-fold increase in the productivity of the MANUAL WORKER in manufacturing.

The most important contribution management needs to make in the 21st century is similarly to increase the productivity of KNOWLEDGE WORK and the KNOWLEDGE WORKER.

The most valuable assets of a 20th-century company were its *production equipment*. The most valuable asset of a 21st-century institution, whether business or nonbusiness, will be its *knowledge workers* and their *productivity*.

I
The Productivity of the Manual Worker

FIRST: a look where we are.

It was only a little over a hundred years ago that for the first time an educated person actually *looked* at manual work and manual worker, and then began to study both. Great poets, the Greek Hesiod (6th century B.C.) and, five hundred years later, the Roman Virgil (at the end of the first century B.C.), sang about the work of the farmer. Theirs are still among the finest poems in any language. But neither the work they sang about nor their farmers bear even the most remote resemblance to reality or were meant to have any. Neither Hesiod nor Virgil ever held a sickle in his hands, ever herded sheep or even looked at the people who did, either. And when, nineteen hundred years after Virgil, Karl Marx (1818–1883) came to write about manual work and manual workers, he too never looked at either, nor had he ever as much as touched a machine. The first man to do both, that is, to work as a manual worker and then to study manual work, was Frederick Winslow Taylor (1856–1915).

Throughout recorded history—and actually well before any history was recorded—there have been, of course, steady advances in what we today call "productivity" (the term itself is barely fifty years old). But they were the result of new tools, of new methods, of new technology; they were advances in what the economist calls "Capital." There were few advances throughout the ages in what the economist calls "Labor," that is, in the productivity of the worker. It was axiomatic throughout history that workers could produce more only by working harder or by working longer hours. The 19th-century economists disagreed as much about most things as economists do today. But they all agreed—from David Ricardo (1772–1823) through Karl Marx—that there are enormous differences in *skill* between workers, but there are none in respect to productivity other than between hard workers and lazy ones, or between physically strong workers and weak ones. Productivity did not exist. It still is an "extraneous factor" and not part of the equation in most contemporary economic theory, for example, in Keynes, but also in that of the Austrian School.

Within a decade after Taylor first looked at work and studied it, the productivity of the manual worker began its unprecedented rise. Since then it has been going up steadily at the rate of 3½ percent per annum compound—which means it has been risen fifty-fold since Taylor. On this achievement rests *all* the economic and social gains of the 20th century. The productivity of the manual worker has created what we now call "developed" economies. Before Taylor there was no such thing—all economies were equally "underdeveloped." An underdeveloped economy today— or even an "emerging" one—is one that has not—or at least has not yet—made the manual worker productive.

The Principles of Manual-Work Productivity

Taylor's principles sound deceptively simple.

> The first step in making the manual worker productive is to look at the task and to analyze its constituent motions.

The next step is to record each motion, the physical effort it takes and the time it takes. Then motions that are not needed can be eliminated—and whenever we have looked at manual work we found that a great many of the traditionally most hallowed procedures turn out to be waste and do not add anything. Then each of the motions that remain as essential to obtaining the finished product is set up so as to be done the simplest way, the easiest way, the way that puts the least physical and mental strain on the operator, the way it requires the least time. Then these motions are put together again into a "job" that is in a logical sequence. Finally the tools needed to do the motions are being redesigned. And whenever we have looked at any job—no matter for how many thousands of years it has been performed—we have found that the traditional tools are totally wrong for the task. This was the case, for instance, with the shovel used to carry sand in a foundry—the first task Taylor studied. It was the wrong shape, it was the wrong size and it had the wrong handle. But we found it to be equally true of the surgeon's traditional tools.

Taylor's principles sound obvious—effective methods always do. But it took Taylor twenty years of experimentation to work them out.

Over these last hundred years there have been countless further changes, revisions and refinements. The name by which the methodology goes has changed too over the century. Taylor himself first called his method "Task Analysis" or "Task Management." Twenty years later it was rechristened "Scientific Management." Another twenty years later, after the First World War, it came to be knows as "Industrial Engineering" in the United States, the United Kingdom and Japan, and as "Rationalization" in Germany.

To proclaim that one's method "rejects" Taylor or "replaces" him is almost standard "Public Relations." For what made Taylor and his method so powerful has also made them unpopular. What Taylor *saw* when he actually looked at work violated everything poets and philosophers had said about work from Hesiod and Virgil to Karl Marx. They all celebrated "skill." Taylor showed that in manual work there is no such thing. There are only simple, repetitive motions. What makes them productive is *knowledge*, that is, the way the simple, unskilled motions are put together, organized and executed. In fact, Taylor was the first person to apply knowledge to work.*

This also earned Taylor the undying enmity of the labor unions of his time, all of which were craft unions and based on the *mystique* of craft skill and their monopoly on it. Moreover, Taylor advocated—and this is still anathema to a labor union—that workers be paid according to their productivity, that is, for their output, rather than for their input, for example, for hours worked. But Taylor's definition of work as a series of operations also largely explains his rejection by the people who themselves do not do any manual work: the descendants of the poets and philosophers of old, the Literati and Intellectuals. Taylor destroyed the romance of work. Instead of a "noble skill" it becomes a series of simple motions.

And yet every method during these last hundred years that has had the slightest success in raising the productivity of manual workers—and with it their real wages—has been based on Taylor's principles, no matter how loudly its protagonists proclaimed their differences with Taylor. This is true of "work enlargement," "work enrichment" and "job rotation"—all of

---

*For work in the oldest knowledge profession, that is, in medicine, Taylor's close contemporary, William Osler (1849-1919), did what Taylor did and at the same time—in his 1892 book *The Principles and Practice of Medicine* (arguably the best textbook since Euclid's *Geometry* in the 3rd century B.C.). Osler's work has rightly been called the application of Scientific Management to Medical Diagnosis. And, like Taylor, Osler preached that there is no "skill," there is only *method*.

which use Taylor's methods to lessen the worker's fatigue and thereby to increase the worker's productivity. It is true of such extensions of Taylor's principles of task analysis and industrial engineering to the entire manual work process as Henry Ford's assembly line (developed after 1914, when Taylor himself was already sick, old and retired). It is just as true of the Japanese "Quality Circle," of "Continuous Improvement" ("Kaizen"), and of "Just-In-Time Delivery."

> The best example, however, is W. Edwards Deming's (1900–1993) "Total Quality Management." What Deming did—and what makes Total Quality Management effective—is to analyze and organize the job exactly the way Taylor did. But then he added, around 1940, Quality Control based on a statistical theory that was only developed ten years after Taylor's death. Finally, in the 1970s, Deming substituted closed-circuit television and computer simulation for Taylor's stopwatch and motion photos. But Deming's Quality Control Analysts are the spit and image of Taylor's Efficiency Engineers and function the same way.

Whatever his limitations and shortcomings—and he had many—no other American, not even Henry Ford (1863–1947), has had anything like Taylor's impact. "Scientific Management" (and its successor, "Industrial Engineering") is the one American philosophy that has swept the world—more so even than the Constitution and the Federalist Papers. In the last century there has been only one worldwide philosophy that could compete with Taylor's: Marxism. And in the end, Taylor has triumphed over Marx.

In the First World War Scientific Management swept through the United States—together with Ford's Taylor-based assembly line. In the twenties Scientific Management swept through Western Europe and began to be adopted in Japan.

In World War II both the German achievement and the American achievement were squarely based on applying Taylor's principles to Training. The German General Staff, after having lost the First World War, applied "Rationalization," that is, Taylor's Scientific Management, to the job of the soldier and to military training. This enabled Hitler to create a superb fighting machine in the six short years between his coming to power and 1939. In the United States, the same principles were applied to the training of an industrial workforce, first tentatively in the First World War, and then, with full power, in WWII. This enabled the Americans to outproduce the Germans, even though a larger proportion of the U.S. than of the German male population was in uniform and thus not in industrial production. And then training-based Scientific Management gave the U.S. civilian workforce more than twice—if not three times—the productivity of the workers in Hitler's Germany and in Hitler-dominated Europe. Scientific Management thus gave the United States the capacity to outnumber both Germans and Japanese on the battlefield and yet to outproduce both by several orders of magnitude.

Economic development outside the Western world since 1950 has largely been based on copying what the United States did in World War II, that is, on applying Scientific Management to making the manual worker productive. All earlier economic development had been based on technological innovation—first in France in the 18th century, then in Great Britain from 1760 until 1850 and finally in the new economic Great Powers, Germany and the United States, in the second half of the 19th century. The non-Western countries that developed after the Second World War, beginning with Japan, eschewed technological innovation. Instead, they imported the training that the United States had developed during the Second World War based on Taylor's principles, and used it to make highly productive, almost overnight, a still largely unskilled and preindustrial workforce. (In Japan, for instance, almost two-thirds of the working population were still, in 1950, living on the land and unskilled in any work except cultivating rice.) But, while highly productive, this new workforce was still—for a decade or more—paid preindustrial wages so that these countries—first Japan, then Korea, then Taiwan and Singapore—could produce the same manufactured products as the developed countries, but at a fraction of their labor costs.

The Future of Manual-Worker Productivity

Taylor's approach was designed for manual work in *manufacturing*, and at first applied only to it. But even within these traditional limitations, it still has enormous scope. It is still going to be the organizing principle in countries in which manual work, and especially manual work in manufacturing, is the growth sector of society and economy, that is, "Third World" countries with very large and still growing numbers of young people with little education and little skill.

But, as will be discussed a little later in this chapter, there is a tremendous amount of knowledge work—including work requiring highly advanced and thoroughly theoretical knowledge—that includes *manual* operations. And the productivity of these operations also requires Industrial Engineering.

Still, in developed countries, the central challenge is no longer to make manual work productive—we know, after all, how to do it. The central challenge will be to make knowledge workers productive. Knowledge workers are rapidly becoming the largest single group in the workforce of every developed country. They may already comprise two-fifths of the U.S. workforce—and a still smaller but rapidly growing proportion of the workforce of all other developed countries. It is on their productivity, above all, that the future prosperity and indeed the future survival of the developed economies will increasingly depend.

II
What We Know About Knowledge-Worker Productivity

Work on the productivity of the knowledge worker has barely begun. In terms of actual work on knowledge worker productivity we are, in the year 2000, roughly where we were in the year 1900, a century ago, in terms of the productivity of the manual worker. But we already know infinitely more about the productivity of the knowledge worker than we did then about that of the manual worker. We even know a good many of the answers. But we also know the challenges to which we do not yet know the answers, and on which we need to go to work.

SIX major factors determine knowledge-worker productivity.

1. Knowledge worker productivity demands that we ask the question: *"What is the task?"*

2. It demands that we impose the responsibility for their productivity on the individual knowledge workers themselves. Knowledge workers *have* to manage themselves. They have to have *autonomy*.

3. Continuing innovation has to be part of the work, the task and the responsibility of knowledge workers.

4. Knowledge work requires continuous learning on the part of the knowledge worker, but equally continuous teaching on the part of the knowledge worker.

5. Productivity of the knowledge worker is not—at least not primarily—a matter of the *quantity* of output. *Quality* is at least as important.

6. Finally, knowledge-worker productivity requires that the knowledge worker is both seen and treated as an "asset" rather than a "cost." It requires that knowledge workers *want* to work for the organization in preference to all other opportunities.

Each of these requirements—except perhaps the last one—is almost the exact opposite of what is needed to increase the productivity of the manual worker.

In manual work quality also matters. But lack of quality is a restraint. There has to be a certain minimum quality standard. The achievement of Total Quality Management, that is, of the application of 20th-century Statistical Theory to manual work, is the ability to cut (though not entirely to eliminate) production that falls below this minimum standard.

But in most knowledge work, quality is not a minimum and a restraint. Quality is the essence of the output. In judging the performance of a teacher, we do not ask how many students there can be in his or her class. We ask how many students learn anything—and that's a quality question. In appraising the performance of a medical laboratory, the question of how many tests it can run through its machines is quite secondary to the question of how many test results are valid and reliable. And this is true even for the work of the file clerk.

Productivity of knowledge work therefore has to aim first at obtaining quality—and not minimum quality but optimum if not maximum quality. Only then can one ask: "What is the volume, the quantity of work?"

This not only means that we approach the task of making productive the knowledge worker from the quality of the work rather than the quantity. It also means that we will have to learn to define quality.

What Is the Task?

But the crucial question in knowledge-worker productivity is the first one: WHAT IS THE TASK? It is also the one most at odds with manual-worker productivity. In manual work the Key Question is always: HOW SHOULD THE WORK BE DONE? In manual work the task is always given. None of the people who work on manual-worker productivity ever asked: "What is the manual worker supposed to do?" Their only question was: "How does the manual worker best do the job?"

This was just as true of Frederick W. Taylor's Scientific Management as it was true of the people at Sears Roebuck or the Ford Motor Company who first designed the assembly line, and of W. Edwards Deming's Total Quality Control.

But in knowledge work the key question is: "What is the task?"

One reason for this is that knowledge work, unlike manual work, does not program the worker. The worker on the automobile assembly line who puts on a wheel is programmed by the simultaneous arrival of the car's chassis on one line and of the wheel on the other line. The farmer who plows a field in preparation for planting does not climb out of his tractor to take a telephone call, to attend a meeting, or to write a memo. *What* is to be done is always obvious in manual work.

But in knowledge work the task does not program the worker.

A major crisis in the hospital, for example, when a patient suddenly goes into coma, does of course control the nurse's task and programs her. But otherwise, it is largely the nurse's decision whether to spend time at the patient's bed or whether to spend time filling out papers. Engineers are constantly being pulled off their task by having to write a report or rewrite it, by being asked to attend a meeting and so on. The job of the salesperson in the department store is to serve the customer and to provide the merchandise the customer is interested in or should become interested in. Instead the salesperson spends an enormous amount of time on paperwork, on checking whether merchandise is in stock, on checking when and how it can be delivered and so on—all things that take salespeople away from the customer and do not add anything to their productivity in doing what salespeople are being paid for, which is to sell and to satisfy the customer.

The first requirement in tackling knowledge work is to find out what the task is so as to make it possible to concentrate knowledge workers on the task and to eliminate everything else— at least as far as it can possibly be eliminated. But this then requires that the knowledge workers themselves define what the task is or should be. And only the knowledge workers themselves can do that.

Work on knowledge-worker productivity therefore begins with asking the knowledge workers themselves:

What is your task? What should it be? What should you be expected to contribute? and What hampers you in doing your task and should be eliminated?

Knowledge workers themselves almost always have thought through these questions and can answer them. Still, it then usually takes time and hard work to restructure their jobs so that they can actually make the contribution they are already being paid for. But asking the questions and taking action on the answers usually doubles or triples knowledge-worker productivity, and quite fast.

This was the result of questioning the nurses in a major hospital. They were actually sharply divided as to what their task was, with one group saying "patient care" and another one saying "satisfying the physicians." But they were in complete agreement on the things that made them unproductive—they called them "chores": paperwork, arranging flowers, answering the phone calls of patients' relatives, answering the patients' bells and so on. And all—or nearly all—of these could be turned over to a nonnurse floor clerk, paid a fraction of a nurse's pay. The productivity of the nurses on the floor immediately more than doubled, as measured by the time nurses spent at the patients' beds. Patient satisfaction more than doubled. And turnover of nurses, which had been catastrophically high, almost disappeared—all within four months.

And once the *task* has been defined, the next requirements can be tackled—and will be tackled by the knowledge workers themselves.

They are:

1. Knowledge workers' *responsibility* for their own contribution—the knowledge worker's decision what he or she should be held accountable for in terms of quality and quantity, in respect to time and in respect to cost. Knowledge workers have to have autonomy, and that entails responsibility.

2. Continuous innovation has to be built into the knowledge worker's job.

3. Continuous learning and continuous teaching have to be built into the job.

These needs have already been discussed in Chapter Three.

But one central requirement of knowledge-worker productivity is then still left to be satisfied. We have to answer the question:

What is quality?

In some knowledge work—and especially in some work requiring a high degree of knowledge—we already measure quality. Surgeons, for instance, are routinely measured, especially by their colleagues, by their success rates in difficult and dangerous procedures, for example, by the survival rates of their open-heart surgical patients or the full recovery rates of their orthopedic-surgery patients. But by and large we have, so far, mainly judgments rather than measures regarding the quality of a great deal of knowledge work. The main trouble is, however, not the difficulty of measuring quality. It is the difficulty—and more particularly the sharp disagreements—in defining what the task is and what it should be.

The best example I know is the American school. As everyone knows, public schools in the American inner city have become disaster areas. But next to them—in the same location and serving the same kind of children—are private (mostly Christian) schools in which the kids behave well and learn well. There is endless speculation to explain these enormous quality differences. But a major reason is surely that the two kinds of schools define their tasks differently. The typical public school defines its task as "helping the underprivileged"; the typical Christian school (and especially the parochial schools of the Catholic church) define their task as "enabling those who want to learn, to learn." One therefore is governed by its scholastic failures, the other one by its scholastic successes.

But similarly: There are two research departments of major pharmaceutical companies that have totally different results because they define their tasks differently. One sees its task as not having failures, that is, in working steadily on fairly minor but predictable improvements in existing products and for established markets. The other one defines its task as producing "breakthroughs" and therefore courts risks. Both are considered fairly successful—by themselves, by their own top managements and by outside analysts. But each operates quite differently and quite differently defines its own productivity and that of its research scientists.

To define quality in knowledge work and to convert the definition into knowledge-worker productivity is thus to a large extent a matter of defining the task. It requires the difficult, risk-taking and always controversial definition as to what "results" are for a given enterprise and a given activity. We therefore actually *know* how to do it. Still, the question is a totally new one for most organizations, and also for most knowledge workers. And to answer it *requires* controversy, *requires* dissent.

The Knowledge Worker as Capital Asset

In no other area is the difference greater between manual-worker productivity and knowledge-worker productivity than in their respective *economics*. Economic theory and most business practice sees manual workers as a *cost*. To be productive, knowledge workers must be considered a *capital asset*.

Costs need to be controlled and reduced. Assets need to be made to grow.

> In managing manual workers we learned fairly early that high turnover, that is, losing workers, is very costly. The Ford Motor Company, as is well known, increased the pay of skilled workers from 80 cents a day to $5 a day in January, 1914. It did so because its turnover had been so excessive as to make its labor costs prohibitively high; it had to hire sixty thousand people a year to keep ten thousand. Even so, everybody, including Henry Ford himself (who had at first been bitterly opposed to this increase) was convinced that the higher wages would greatly reduce the company's profits. Instead, in the very first year, profits almost doubled. Paid $5 a day, practically no workers left—in fact, the Ford Motor Company soon had a waiting list.

But, short of the costs of turnover, rehiring or retraining and so on, the manual worker is still being seen as a cost. This is true even in Japan, despite the emphasis on lifetime employment and on building a "loyal," permanent workforce. And short of the cost of turnover, the management of people at work, based on millennia of work being almost totally manual work, still assumes that with the exception of a few highly skilled people one manual worker is like any other manual worker.

This is definitely not true for knowledge work.

Employees who do manual work do not own the means of production. They may, and often do, have a lot of valuable experience. But that experience is valuable only at the place where they work. It is not portable.

But knowledge workers *own* the means of production. It is the knowledge between their ears. And it is a totally portable and enormous capital asset. Because knowledge workers own their means of production, they are mobile. Manual workers need the job much more than the job needs them. It may still not be true for all knowledge workers that the organization needs them more than they need the organization. But for most of them it is a symbiotic relationship in which they need each other in equal measure.

Management's duty is to preserve the assets of the institution in its care. What does this mean when the knowledge of the individual knowledge worker becomes an asset and, in more and more cases, the *main* asset of an institution? What does this mean for personnel policy? What is needed to attract and to hold the highest-producing knowledge workers? What is needed to increase their productivity and to convert their increased productivity into performance capacity for the organization?

III
The Technologists

So far we have discussed the productivity of knowledge workers doing knowledge work. But a very large number of knowledge workers do both knowledge work *and* manual work. I call them "technologists."

This group includes people who apply knowledge of the highest order.

Surgeons preparing for an operation to correct a brain aneurysm before it produces a lethal brain hemorrhage spend hours in diagnosis *before* they cut—and that requires specialized knowledge of the highest order. And then again, during the surgery, an unexpected complication may occur that calls for theoretical knowledge and judgment, both of the very highest order. But the surgery itself is manual work—and manual work consisting of repetitive manual operations in which the emphasis is on speed, accuracy, uniformity. And these operations are studied, organized, learned and practiced exactly like any manual work, that is, by the same methods Taylor first developed for factory work.

But the technologist group also contains large numbers of people in whose work knowledge is relatively subordinate—though it is always crucial.

The file clerk's job—and that of her computer-operator successor—requires knowledge of the alphabet that no experience can teach. This knowledge is a small part of an otherwise manual task. But it is the foundation and absolutely crucial.

Technologists may be the single biggest group of knowledge workers. They may also be the fastest-growing group. They include the great majority of health care workers: lab technicians; rehabilitation technicians; technicians in imaging such as X-ray, ultrasound, magnetic-resonance imaging, and so on. They include dentists and all dental support people. They include automobile mechanics and all kinds of repair and installation people. In fact, the technologist may be the true successor to the 19th- and 20th-century skilled workers.

Technologists are also the one group in which developed countries can have a true and long-lasting competitive advantage.

When it comes to truly high knowledge, no country can any longer have much of a lead, the way 19th-century

Germany had through its university. Among theoretical physicists, mathematicians, economic theorists and the like, there is no "nationality." And any country can, at fairly low cost, train a substantial number of high-knowledge people. India, for instance, despite her poverty, has been training fairly large numbers of first-rate physicians and first-rate computer programmers. Similarly (as discussed earlier in this chapter), there is no "nationality" in respect to the productivity of manual labor. Training based on Scientific Management has made all countries capable of attaining, overnight, the manual-worker productivity of the most advanced country, industry or company. Only in educating technologists can the developed countries still have a meaningful competitive edge, and for some time to come.

The United States is the only country that has actually developed this advantage—through its so far unique nationwide systems of community colleges. The community college was actually *designed* (beginning in the 1920s) to educate technologists who have *both* the needed theoretical knowledge *and* the manual skill. On this, I am convinced, rests both the still huge productivity advantage of the American economy and the—so far unique—American ability to create, almost overnight, new and different industries.

Nothing quite like the American community college exists anywhere else so far. The famous Japanese school system produces either people prepared only for manual work or people prepared only for knowledge work. Only in the year 2003 is the first Japanese institution devoted to training technologists supposed to get started. Even more famous is the German apprenticeship system. Started in the 1830s, it was one of the main factors in Germany's becoming the world's leading manufacturer. But it focused—and still focuses—primarily on manual skills and slights theoretical knowledge. It is thus in danger of becoming rapidly obsolete.

But these other developed countries should be expected to catch up with the United States fairly fast. Other countries—"emerging ones" or "Third World" ones—are, however, likely to be decades behind—in part because educating technologists is expensive, in part because in these countries people of knowledge still look down with disdain, if not with contempt, on working with one's hands. "That's what we have servants for," is still their prevailing attitude. In developed countries, however—and again foremost in the United States—more and more manual workers are going to be technologists. In increasing knowledge-worker productivity, increasing the productivity of the technologists therefore deserves to be given high priority.

The job was actually done—more than seventy years ago—by the American Telephone Company (AT&T) for its technologists, the people who install, maintain, replace telephones, whether in the home or in the office.

By the early 1920s the technologists working outside the telephone office and at the customer's location had become a major cost center—and at the same time a major cause of customer unhappiness and dissatisfaction. It took about five years or so, from 1920 until 1925, for AT&T—which had by that time acquired a near monopoly on providing telephone service in the United States and in parts of Canada—to realize that the task was not installing, maintaining, repairing and replacing telephones and telephone connections. *The task was to create a satisfied customer*. It became fairly easy to organize the job. It meant, first, that the technicians themselves had to define what "satisfaction" meant. The results were standards that established that every order for a new telephone or an additional telephone connection would have to be satisfied within at most forty-eight hours, and that every request for repair would have to be satisfied the same day if made before noon, or by noon the following day. Then it became clear that the individual service people—in those days all men, of course—would have to be active participants in such decisions as whether to have one person installing and replacing telephones, and another one maintaining and repairing them, or whether the same people had to be able to do all jobs—which in the end turned out to be the right answer. These people had to be taught a very substantial amount of theoretical knowledge—and in those days few of them had more than six years of schooling. They had to understand how a telephone works. They had to understand how a switchboard works. They had to understand how the telephone system works. These people were not qualified engineers or skilled craftsmen. But they had to know enough electronics to diagnose unexpected problems and to be able to cope with them. Then they were trained in the repetitive manual operation or in the "one right way," that is, through the methods of Scientific Management. And *they* made the decisions, for example, where and how to connect the individual telephone to the system, and what particular kind of telephone and service would be the most suitable for a given home or a given office. They had to become salesmen in addition to being servicemen.

Finally, the telephone company faced the problem of how to define *quality*. The technologist had to work by himself. He could not be supervised. He, therefore, had to define quality and had to deliver it. It took several more years before that was answered. At first the telephone company thought that this meant a sample check that had supervisors go out and look at a sample—maybe every twentieth or thirtieth job done by an individual service person—and check it for quality. This very soon turned out to be the wrong way of doing the job, annoying both servicemen and customers alike. Then the telephone company defined quality as "no complaints"—and soon found out that only extremely unhappy customers complained. It then had to redefine quality as "positive customer satisfaction." And this then meant in the end that the serviceman himself controlled quality—for example, by calling up a week or ten days after he had done a job and asking the customer whether the work was satisfactory and whether there was anything more the technician could possibly do to give the customer the best possible and most satisfactory service.

I have intentionally gone into considerable detail in describing this early example because it exemplifies the three elements for making effective the worker who is both a knowledge worker and a manual worker.

1. There is, first, the answer to the question: "What is the task?"—the key question in making every knowledge worker productive. As the example of the Bell System shows, this is not an obvious answer. And as the Bell System people learned, the only people who know the answer to this are the technologists themselves. In fact, until they asked the technologists, they floundered. But as soon as the technologists were asked, the answer came back loud and clear: a satisfied customer.

2. Then the technologists had to take full responsibility for giving customer satisfaction, that is, for delivering quality. This then showed what *formal knowledge* the technologist needed. And then, only then, could the *manual* part of the job be organized for manual-worker productivity.

3. Above all, this example shows that technologists have to be treated as *knowledge workers*. No matter how important the manual part of their work—and it may take the bulk of their time, as it did in the case of the AT&T installers—the focus has to be on making the technologist knowledgeable, responsible, productive as a knowledge worker.

IV
Knowledge Work as a System

Productivity of the knowledge worker will almost always require that the *work itself* be restructured and be made part of a *system*.

One example is servicing expensive equipment, such as huge and expensive earth-moving machines. Traditionally, this had been seen as distinct and separate from the job of making and selling the machines. But when the U.S. Caterpillar Company, the world's largest producer of such equipment, asked "What are we getting paid for?" the answer was, "We are not getting paid for machinery. We are getting paid for what the machinery does at the customer's place of business. That means keeping the equipment running, since even one hour during which the equipment is out of operation may cost the customer far more than the equipment itself." In other words, the answer to "What is our business?" was "Service." This then led to a total restructuring of operations all the way back to the factory, so that the customer can be guaranteed continuing operations and immediate repairs or replacements. And the service representative, usually a technologist, has become the true "decision maker."

Another example. A group of about twenty-five orthopedic surgeons in a Midwestern U.S. city have organized themselves as a "system" to produce highest-quality work: to use optimally the limited and expensive resources of operating and recovery rooms; to use optimally the supporting knowledge people such as anesthesiologists or surgical nurses; to build in continuous learning and continuous innovation into the work of the entire group and of every member thereof; and finally, to minimize costs. Each of the surgeons retains full control of his or her practice. He or she is fully responsible for obtaining and treating the individual patient. Traditionally each surgeon schedules surgeries early in the morning. Hence, operating rooms and recovery rooms are standing empty most of the time. The group now schedules the use of operating and recovery rooms for the entire group so that this scarce and extremely expensive resource is used ten hours a day. The group, as a group, decides on the standardization of tools and equipment so as to obtain the highest quality at the lowest cost. Finally, the group has also built quality control into its system. Every three months three different surgeons are designated to scrutinize every operation done by each of the members—the diagnosis, the surgery, the after-treatment. They then sit down with the individual surgeons and discuss their performance. They suggest where there is need for improvement. But they also may recommend that a certain surgeon be asked to leave the group, as his or her work is not satisfactory. And each year the quality standards that these supervising committees apply are discussed with the whole group and are raised, and often substantially. As a result this group now does almost four times as much work as it did before. It has cut the costs by 50 percent, half of it by cutting back on the waste of operating and recovery rooms, half by standardizing tools and equipment. And in such measurable areas as success rates in knee replacements or shoulder replacements, or in recovery after sports injuries, it has greatly improved its results.

What to do about knowledge worker productivity is thus largely known. So is *how* to do it.

But How to Begin?

Making knowledge workers productive requires changes in basic attitude—whereas making the manual worker more productive only required telling the worker how to do the job. And making knowledge workers productive requires changes in attitude, not only on the part of the individual knowledge worker but on the part of the whole organization. It therefore has to be "piloted"—as any major change should be (on this see Chapter Three). The first step is to find an area in the organization or a group of knowledge workers who are receptive. The orthopedic surgeons, for instance, first had their new ideas tried out by four physicians— one an older man, three younger people—who had long argued for radical changes. Then there is a need to work consistently, patiently, and for a considerable length of uninterrupted time, in this small area or with this small group. For the first attempts, even if greeted with great enthusiasm, will almost certainly run into all kinds of unexpected problems. It is only after the productivity of this small group of knowledge workers has been substantially increased that the new ways of doing the work can be extended to a larger area, if not to the entire organization. And by then we will also have learned where the main problems are; where, for example, resistance can be expected (e.g., from middle management), or what changes in task, organization, measurements and attitudes are needed for full effectiveness. To try to jump the pilot stage—and there is always pressure to do so—only means that the mistakes become public, while the successes stay hidden. It only means discrediting the entire enterprise. But if properly piloted, we can already do a great deal to improve—and drastically—knowledge-worker productivity.

Knowledge-worker productivity is the biggest of the 21st-century management challenges. In the developed countries it is their first *survival requirement*. In no other way can the developed countries hope to maintain themselves, let alone to maintain their leadership and their standards of living.

In the last hundred years, that is, in the 20th century, this leadership very largely depended on making the manual worker productive. Any country, any industry, any business can do that today—using the methods that the developed countries have worked out and put into practice in the 120 years since Frederick Winslow Taylor first looked at manual work. Anybody today, any-place, can apply those policies to training, to the organization of the work and to the productivity of workers, even if they are barely literate, if not illiterate, and totally unskilled.

Above all (as discussed in Chapter Two), the supply of young people available for manual work will be rapidly shrinking in the developed countries—in the West and in Japan very fast, in the United States somewhat more slowly—whereas the supply of such people will still grow fast in the emerging and developing countries, at least for another thirty or forty years. The only possible advantage developed countries can hope to have is in the supply of people prepared, educated and trained for knowledge work. There, for another fifty years, the developed countries can expect to have substantial advantages, both in quality and in quantity.

But whether this advantage will translate into performance depends on the ability of the developed countries—and of every industry in it, of every company in it, of every institution in it—to raise the productivity of the knowledge worker and to raise it as fast as the developed countries, in the last hundred years, have raised the productivity of the manual worker.

The countries and the industries that have emerged as the leaders in the last hundred years in the world are the countries and the industries that have led in raising the productivity of the manual worker: the United States first, Japan and Germany second. Fifty years from now—if not much sooner—the leadership in the world economy will have moved to the countries and to the industries that have most systematically and most successfully raised knowledge-worker productivity.

V
The Governance of the Corporation

What does the emergence of the knowledge worker and of knowledge-worker productivity mean for the *governance of the corporation*? What do they mean for the future and structure of the economic system?

In the last ten or fifteen years pension funds and other institutional investors became the main share owners of the equity capital of publicly owned companies in all developed countries (as discussed several times in this book). This has triggered in the United States a furious debate on the governance of corporations (on this see also Chapters One and Two). For with the emergence of pension funds and mutual funds as the owners of publicly owned companies, power has shifted to these new owners.

Similar shifts in both the definition of the purpose of economic organizations such as the business corporation, and of their governance, can be expected to occur in all developed countries.

But within a fairly short period of time, we will face the problem of the governance of corporations again. We will have to redefine the purpose of the employing organization and of its management as *both*, satisfying the legal owners, such as shareholders, and satisfying the owners of the human capital that gives the organization its wealth-producing power, that is, satisfying the knowledge workers. For increasingly the ability of organizations—and not only of businesses—to survive will come to depend on their "comparative advantage" in making the knowledge worker productive. And the ability to attract and hold the best of the knowledge workers is the first and most fundamental precondition.

Can this be *measured*, however? Or is it purely an "intangible"? This will surely be a central problem—for management, for investors, for capital markets. What does "Capitalism" mean when Knowledge governs—rather than Money? And what do "Free Markets" mean when knowledge workers—and no one else can "own" knowledge—are the true assets? Knowledge workers can be neither bought nor sold. They do not come with a merger or an acquisition. In fact, though the greatest "value," they have no "market value"—that means, of course, that they are not an "asset" in any sense of the term.

These questions go far beyond the scope of this book—let alone far beyond the author's competence. But it is certain that the emergence of the knowledge worker and of the knowledge worker's productivity as *key questions* will, within a few decades, bring about fundamental changes in the very structure and nature of THE ECONOMIC SYSTEM.

6
Managing Oneself

What Are My Strengths? · How Do I Perform? · Where
Do I Belong? · What Is *My* Contribution? · Relationship
Responsibility · The Second Half of Your Life · The
Parallel Career

Introduction

More and more people in the workforce—and most knowledge workers—will have to MANAGE THEMSELVES. They will have to place themselves where they can make the greatest contribution; they will have to learn to develop themselves. They will have to learn to stay young and mentally alive during a fifty-year working life. They will have to learn how and when to change what they do, how they do it and when they do it.

Knowledge workers are likely to outlive their employing organization. Even if knowledge workers postpone entry into the labor force as long as possible—if, for instance, they stay in school till their late twenties to get a doctorate—they are likely, with present life expectancies in the developed countries, to live into their eighties. And they are likely to have to keep working, if only part-time, until they are around seventy-five or older. The average working life, in other words, is likely to be fifty years, especially for knowledge workers. But the average life expectancy of a successful business is only thirty years—and in a period of great turbulence such as the one we are living in, it is unlikely to be even that long. Even organizations that normally are long-lived if not expected to live forever—schools and universities, hospitals, government agencies—will see rapid changes in the period of turbulence we have already entered. Even if they survive—and a great many surely will not, at least not in their present form—they will change their structure, the work they are doing, the knowledges they require and the kind of people they employ. Increasingly, therefore, workers, and especially knowledge workers, will outlive any one employer, and will have to be prepared for more than one job, more than one assignment, more than one career.

So far, this book has dealt with changes in the environment: in society, economy, politics, technology. *This concluding chapter deals with the new demands on the individual.*

The very great achievers, a Napoleon, a Leonardo da Vinci, a Mozart, have always managed themselves. This in large measure made them great achievers. But they were the rarest of exceptions. And they were so unusual, both in their talents and in their achievements, as to be considered outside the boundaries of normal human existence. Now even people of modest endowments, that is, average mediocrities, will have to learn to manage themselves.

Knowledge workers, therefore, face drastically new demands:

1. They have to ask: Who Am I? What Are My Strengths? *HOW* Do I Work?

2. They have to ask: Where Do I Belong?

3. They have to ask: What Is My Contribution?

4. They have to take Relationship Responsibility.

5. They have to plan for the Second Half of Their Lives.

I
What Are My Strengths?

Most people think they know what they are good at. They are usually wrong. People know what they are *not* good at more often—and even there people are more often wrong than right. And yet, one can only perform with one's strengths. One cannot build performance on weaknesses, let alone on something one cannot do at all.

For the great majority of people, to know their strengths was irrelevant only a few decades ago. One was born into a job and into a line of work. The peasant's son became a peasant. If he was not good at being a peasant, he failed. The artisan's son was similarly going to be an artisan, and so on. But now people have choices. They therefore have to know their strengths so that they can know where they belong.

There is only one way to find out: *The Feedback Analysis*. Whenever one makes a key decision, and whenever one does a key action, one writes down what one expects will happen. And nine months or twelve months later one then feeds back from results to expectations. I have been doing this for some fifteen to twenty years now. And every time I do it I am surprised. And so is everyone who has ever done this.

This is by no means a new method. It was invented sometime in the 14th century, by an otherwise totally obscure German theologian. Some 150 years later Jean Calvin in Geneva (1509–1564), father of Calvinism, and Ignatius Loyola (1491–1556), the founder of the Jesuit Order, quite independent of each other, picked up the idea and incorporated it into their rules for every member of their groups, that is, for the Calvinist pastor and the Jesuit priest. This explains why these two new institutions (both founded in the same year, in 1536) had come within thirty years to dominate Europe: Calvinism the Protestant north; the Jesuit Order the Catholic south. By that time each group contained so many thousands of members that most of them had to be ordinary rather than exceptional. Many of them worked alone, if not in complete isolation. Many of them had to work underground and in constant fear of persecution. Yet very few defected. The routine feedback from results to expectations reaffirmed them in their commitment. It enabled them to focus on performance and results, and with it, on achievement and satisfaction.

Within a fairly short period of time, maybe two or three years, this simple procedure will tell people first where their strengths are—and this is probably the most important thing to know about oneself. It will show them what they do or fail to do that deprives them of the full yield from their strengths. It will show them where they are not particularly competent. And it will finally show them where they have no strengths and cannot perform.

Several *action conclusions* follow from the feedback analysis.

The first, and most important, conclusion: *Concentrate on your strengths*. Place yourself where your strengths can produce performance and results.

Second: Work on improving your strengths. The feedback analysis rapidly shows where a person needs to improve skills or has to acquire new knowledge. It will show where skills and knowledge are no longer adequate and have to be updated. It will also show the gaps in one's knowledge.

And one can usually acquire enough of any skill or knowledge not to be incompetent in it.

> Mathematicians are born. But almost everyone can learn trigonometry. And the same holds for foreign languages or for major disciplines, whether history or economics or chemistry.

Of particular importance is the third conclusion: the feedback analysis soon identifies the areas where intellectual arrogance causes *disabling ignorance*. Far too many people—and especially people with high knowledge in one area—are contemptuous of knowledge in other areas or believe that being "bright" is a substitute for knowing. And then the feedback analysis soon shows that a main reason for poor performance is the result of simply not knowing enough, or the result of being contemptuous of knowledge outside one's own specialty.

> First-rate engineers tend to take pride in not knowing anything about people—human beings are much too disorderly for the good engineering mind. And accountants, too, tend to think it unnecessary to know about people. Human Resources people, by contrast, often pride themselves of their ignorance of elementary accounting or of quantitative methods altogether. Brilliant executives who are being posted abroad often believe that business skill is sufficient, and dismiss learning about the history, the arts, the culture, the traditions of the country where they are now expected to perform—only to find that their brilliant business skills produce no results.

One important action conclusion from the feedback analysis is thus to overcome intellectual arrogance and work on acquiring the skills and knowledge needed to make one's strengths fully productive.

An equally important action conclusion is to remedy one's *bad habits*—things one does or fails to do that inhibit effectiveness and performance. They quickly show up in the feedback analysis.

The analysis may show, for instance, that a planner's beautiful plans die because he or she does not follow through. Like so many brilliant people, he or she believes that ideas move mountains. But bulldozers move mountains; ideas show where the bulldozers have to go to work. The most brilliant planners far too often stop when the plan is completed. But that is when the *work* begins. Then the planner needs to find the people to carry out the plan, explain the plan to them, teach them, adapt and change the plan as it moves from planning to doing and, finally, decide when to stop pushing the plan.

But the analysis may also show that a person fails to obtain results because he or she lacks *manners*. Bright people—especially bright young people—often do not understand that manners are the "lubricating oil" of an organization.

It is a Law of Nature that two moving bodies in contact with each other create friction. Two human beings in contact with each other therefore always create friction. And then manners are the lubricating oil that enables these two moving bodies to work together, whether they like each other or not—simple things like saying "please" and "thank you" and knowing a person's birthday or name, and remembering to ask after the person's family. If the analysis shows that brilliant work fails again and again as soon as it requires cooperation by others, it probably indicates a lack of courtesy, that is, of manners.

The next action conclusion from the feedback analysis is what *not* to do.

Feeding back from results to expectations soon shows where a person should not try to do anything at all. It shows the areas in which a person lacks the minimum endowment needed—and there are always many such areas for any person. Not enough people have even one first-rate skill or knowledge area, but all of us have an infinite number of areas in which we have no talent, no skill and little chance to become even mediocre. And in these areas a person—and especially a knowledge worker—should not take on work, jobs, assignments.

The final action conclusion is to waste as little effort as possible on improving areas of low competence. Concentration should be on areas of high competence and high skill. It takes far more energy and far more work to improve from incompetence to low mediocrity than it takes to improve from first-rate performance to excellence. And yet most people—and equally most teachers and most organizations—try to concentrate on making an incompetent person into a low mediocrity. The energy and resources—and time—should instead go into making a competent person into a star performer.

How Do I Perform?

How Do I Perform? is as important a question—and especially for knowledge workers—as What Are My Strengths?

In fact, it may be an even more important question. Amazingly few people know *how* they get things done. On the contrary, most of us do not even know that different people work and perform differently. They therefore work in ways that are not their ways—and that almost guarantees nonperformance.

The main reason perhaps that so many people do not know how they perform is that the schools throughout history insisted out of necessity on there being only one way for everybody to do his or her schoolwork. The teacher who ran a classroom of forty youngsters simply did not have the time to find out how each of the students performed. The teacher, on the contrary, had to insist that all do the same work, the same way, the same time. And so historically everybody grew up with one way of doing the work. Here perhaps is where the new technology may have the greatest and most beneficial impact. It should enable even the merely competent teacher to find out how a student learns and then to encourage the student to do the work the way that fits the individual student.

Like one's strengths, how one performs is *individual*. It is *personality*. Whether personality be "nature" or "nurture," it surely is formed long before the person goes to work. And *how* a person performs is a "given," just as *what* a person is good at or not good at is a "given." It can be modified, but it is unlikely to be changed. And just as people have results by doing *what* they are good at, people have results by performing *how* they perform.

The feedback analysis may indicate that there is something amiss in how one performs. But rarely does it identify the cause. It is, however, normally not too difficult to find out. It takes a few years of work experience. And then one can ask—and quickly answer—*how* one performs. For a few common personality traits usually determine how one achieves results.

Am I a Reader or a Listener?

The first thing to know about how one performs is whether one is a reader or a listener. Yet very few people even know that there are readers and there are listeners, and that very few people are both. Even fewer know which of the two they themselves are. But a few examples will show how damaging it is not to know.

When he was Commander-in-Chief of the Allied Forces in Europe, *General* Dwight (Ike) Eisenhower was the darling

of the press, and attendance at one of his press conferences was considered a rare treat. These conferences were
famous for their style, for Eisenhower's total command of
whatever question was being asked and, equally, for his
ability to describe a situation or to explain a policy in two
or three beautifully polished and elegant sentences. Ten
years later, *President* Eisenhower was held in open contempt by his former admirers. They considered him a buf-
foon. He never, they complained, even addressed himself
to the question asked, but rambled on endlessly about
something else. And he was constantly ridiculed for
butchering the King's English in his incoherent and
ungrammatical answers. Yet Eisenhower had owed his
brilliant earlier career in large measure to a virtuoso performance as a speechwriter for General MacArthur, one of
the most demanding stylists in American public life.

The explanation: Eisenhower apparently did not know himself that he was a *reader* and not a listener. When he was
Commander-in-Chief in Europe, his aides made sure that every
question from the press was handed in *in writing* at least half an
hour before the conference began. And then Eisenhower was in
total command. When he became President he succeeded two listeners, Franklin D. Roosevelt and Harry Truman. Both men knew
this and both enjoyed free-for-all press conferences. Roosevelt
knew himself to be so much of a listener that he insisted that
everything first be read out loud to him—only then did he look at
anything in writing. And when Truman realized, after becoming
President, that he needed to learn about foreign and military
affairs—neither of which he had ever been much interested in
before—he arranged for his two ablest Cabinet members, General
Marshall and Dean Acheson, to give him a daily tutorial in which
each delivered a forty-minute *spoken* presentation, after which the
President asked questions. Eisenhower, apparently, felt that he
had to do what his two famous predecessors had done. As a
result, he never even heard the question the journalists asked.
And he was not even an extreme case of a nonlistener.

A few years later Lyndon Johnson destroyed his Presidency, in large measure, by not knowing that he—unlike Eisenhower—was a listener. His predecessor, John Kennedy, who knew that he was a reader, had assembled as his assistants a brilliant group of *writers* such as Arthur Schlesinger, Jr., the historian, and Bill Moyers, a first-rate journalist. Kennedy made sure that they first wrote to him before discussing their memos in person. Johnson kept these people as his staff—and they kept on writing. He never, apparently, got one word of what they wrote. Yet, as a senator, Johnson, only four years earlier, had been superb; for parliamentarians have, above all, to be listeners.

Only a century ago very few people, even in the most highly developed country, knew whether they were right-handed or left-handed. Left-handers were suppressed. Few actually became competent right-handers. Most of them ended up as incompetent no-handers and with severe emotional damage such as stuttering.

But only one of every ten human beings is left-handed. The ratio of listeners to readers seems, however, to be close to fifty-fifty. Yet, just as few left-handers became competent right-handers, few listeners can be made, or can make themselves, into competent readers—and vice versa.

The listener who tries to be a reader will, therefore, suffer the fate of Lyndon Johnson, while the reader who tries to be a listener will suffer the fate of Dwight Eisenhower. They will not perform or achieve.

How Do I Learn?

The second thing to know about how one performs is to know how one *learns*. There things may be even worse than they are in respect to readers and listeners. For schools everywhere are organized on the assumption that there is one right way to learn, and that it is the same way for everybody.

Many first-class writers—Winston Churchill is but one example—do poorly in school, and they tend to remember their school as pure torture. Yet few of their classmates have the same memory of the same school and the same teachers; they may not have enjoyed the school very much but the worst they suffered was boredom. The explanation is that first-rate writers do not, as a rule, learn by listening and reading. They learn by writing. Since this is not the way the school allows them to learn, they get poor grades. And to be forced to learn the way the school teaches is sheer hell for them and pure torture.

Here are a few examples of different ways in which people learn.

Beethoven left behind an enormous number of sketchbooks. Yet he himself said that he never looked at a sketchbook when he actually wrote his compositions. When asked, "Why then, do you keep a sketchbook?" he is reported to have answered, "If I don't write it down immediately I forget it right away. If I put it into a sketchbook I never forget it, and I never have to look it up again."

Alfred Sloan—the man who built General Motors into the world's largest, and for sixty years the world's most successful, manufacturing company—conducted most of his management business in small and lively meetings. As soon as a meeting was over, Sloan went to his office and spent several hours composing a letter to one of the meeting's participants, in which he brought out the key questions discussed in the meeting, the issues the meeting raised, the decisions it reached and the problems it uncovered but did not solve. When complimented on these letters, he is reported to have said, "If I do not sit down immediately after the meeting and think through what it actually was all about, and then put it down in writing, I will have forgotten it within twenty-four hours. That's why I write these letters."

• • •

A chief executive officer who, in the 1950s and 1960s, converted what was a small and mediocre family firm into the world's leading company in its industry, was in the habit of calling his entire senior staff into his office, usually once a week, having them sit in a half-circle around his desk, and then talking *at* them for two or three hours. He very rarely asked these people for their comments or their questions. He argued with himself. He raised the possibility of a policy move—acquisition of a small and failing company in the industry that had, however, some special technology, for instance. He always took three different positions on every one of these questions: one in favor of the move, one against the move and one on the conditions under which such a move might make sense. *He needed an audience to hear himself talk.* It was the way he learned. And again, while a fairly extreme case, he was by no means an unusual one. Successful trial lawyers learn the same way; so do many medical diagnosticians.

There are probably half a dozen different ways to learn. There are people who learn by taking copious notes—the way Beethoven did. But Alfred Sloan never took a note in a meeting, nor did the CEO mentioned above. There are people who learn by hearing themselves talk. There are people who learn by writing. There are people who learn by doing. And in an (informal) survey I once took of professors in American universities who successfully publish scholarly books of wide appeal, I was told again and again, "To hear myself talk is the reason why I teach; because then I can write."

Actually, of all the important pieces of self-knowledge, this is one of the easiest to acquire. When I ask people, "How do you learn?" most of them know it. But when I then ask, "Do you act on this knowledge?" few do. And yet to act on this knowledge is the key to performance—or rather *not* to act on this knowledge is to condemn oneself to nonperformance.

To ask "How do I perform?" and "How do I learn?" are the most important first questions to ask. But they are by no means the only ones. To manage oneself one has to ask: "Do I work well with people, or am I a loner?" And if one finds out that one works well with people, one asks: "In what relationship do I work well with people?"

Some people work best as subordinates.

> The prime example is the great American military hero of World War II, General George Patton. He was America's top troop commander. Yet, when he was proposed for an independent command, General George Marshall, the American Chief of Staff—and probably the most successful picker of men in American history—said: "Patton is the best subordinate the American Army has ever produced, but he would be the worst commander."

Some people work best as team members. Some people work exceedingly well as coaches and mentors, and some people are simply incompetent to be mentors.

Another important thing to know about how one performs is whether one performs well under *stress*, or whether one needs a highly structured and predictable environment. Another trait: Does one work best as a minnow in a big organization, or best as a big fish in a small organization? Few people work well in both ways. Again and again people who have been very successful in a large organization—for example, the General Electric Company or Citibank—flounder miserably when they move into a small organization. And again and again people who perform brilliantly in a small organization flounder miserably when they take a job with a big organization.

Another crucial question: "Do I produce results as a decision maker or as an adviser?" A great many people perform best as advisers, but cannot take the burden and pressure of the decision. A good many people, by contrast, need an adviser to force themselves to think, but then they can take the decision and act on it with speed, self-confidence and courage.

> This is a reason, by the way, why the number-two person in an organization often fails when promoted into the top spot. The top spot requires a decision maker. Strong decision makers in the top spot often put somebody whom

they trust into the number-two spot as their adviser—and in that position that person is outstanding. But when then promoted into the number-one spot, the person fails. He or she knows what the decision should be but cannot take decision-*making* responsibility.

The *action conclusion*: Again, do not try to change yourself—it is unlikely to be successful. But work, and hard, to improve the way you perform. And try not to do work of any kind in a way you do not perform or perform poorly.

What Are My Values?

To be able to manage oneself, one finally has to know: "What are my values?"

In respect to *ethics*, the rules are the same for everybody, and the test is a simple one—I call it the "*mirror test*."

As the story goes, the most highly respected diplomatist of all the Great Powers in the early years of this century was the German Ambassador in London. He was clearly destined for higher things, at least to become his country's Foreign Minister, if not German Federal Chancellor. Yet, in 1906, he abruptly resigned. King Edward VII had then been on the British throne for five years, and the diplomatic corps was going to give him a big dinner. The German ambassador, being the dean of the diplomatic corps—he had been in London for close to fifteen years—was to be the chairman of that dinner. King Edward VII was a notorious womanizer and made it clear what kind of dinner he wanted—at the end, after the desert had been served, a huge cake was going to appear, and out of it would jump a dozen or more naked prostitutes as the lights were dimmed. And the German ambassador resigned rather than preside over this dinner. "I refuse to see a pimp in the mirror in the morning, when I shave."

This is the mirror test. What ethics requires is to ask oneself: "What kind of person do I want to see when I shave myself in the morning, or put on my lipstick in the morning?" Ethics, in other words, are a clear value system. And they do not vary much—what is ethical behavior in one kind of organization or situation is ethical behavior in another kind of organization or situation.

But ethics are only a part of the value system and, especially, only a part of the value system of an organization.

To work in an organization the value system of which is unacceptable to a person, or incompatible with it, condemns the person both to frustration and to nonperformance.

Here are some examples of values people have to learn about themselves.

A brilliant and highly successful executive found herself totally frustrated after her old company was acquired by a bigger one. She actually got a big promotion—and a promotion into doing the kind of work she did best. It was part of her job to select people for important positions. She deeply believed that one only hired people from the outside into important positions after having exhausted all inside possibilities. The company in which she now found herself as a senior human resources executive believed, however, that in staffing an important position that had become vacant, one first looked at the outside, "to bring in fresh blood." There is something to be said for either way (though, in my experience, the proper one is to do some of both). But they are fundamentally incompatible, not as policies but as values. They bespeak a different view of the relationship between organization and people; a different view of the responsibility of an organization to its people and in respect to developing them; a different view in what is the most important contribution of a person to an enterprise, and so on. After several years of frustration, the human resources executive quit, at considerable financial loss to herself. Her values and the values of the organization simply were not compatible.

Similarly, whether to try to obtain results in a pharmaceutical company by making constant, small improvements, or by occasional, highly expensive and risky "breakthroughs" is not primarily an economic question. The results of either strategy may be pretty much the same. It is at bottom a conflict of values—between a value system that sees the contribution of a pharmaceutical company to help the already successful physician to do better what he or she already does well, and a value system that is "science" oriented.

It is similarly a value question whether a business should be run for short-term results or for "the long run." Financial analysts believe that businesses can be run for both, simultaneously. Successful businessmen know better. To be sure, everyone has to produce short-term results. But in any conflict between short-term results and long-term growth, one company decides in favor of long-term growth; another company decides such a conflict in favor of short-term results. Again, this is not primarily a disagreement on economics. It is fundamentally a value conflict regarding the function of a business and the responsibility of management.

In one of the fastest-growing pastoral churches in the United States, success is being measured by the number of new parishioners. It is believed that what matters is how many people join, and become regular churchgoers, who never before came to church. The Good Lord, this church believes, will then take care of the spiritual needs of a sufficient number. Another pastoral, evangelical church believes that what matters is the spiritual experience of people. It will ease out newcomers who join the church but who then do not enter into the spiritual life of the church.

Again, this is not a matter of numbers. At first glance it appears that the second church grows more slowly. But it retains a far larger proportion of newcomers than the first one does. Its growth, in other words, is far more solid. This is also not a theological problem, or only secondarily so. It is a *value problem*. One of the two pastors said in a public debate, "Unless you first come to church you will never find the Gate to the Kingdom of Heaven." "No," answered the other one. "Until you first look for the Gate to the Kingdom of Heaven, you don't belong in church."

Organizations have to have values. But so do people. To be effective in an organization, one's own values must be compatible with the organization's values. They do not need to be the same. But they must be close enough so that they can coexist. Otherwise, the person will be frustrated, but also the person will not produce results.

What to Do in a Value Conflict?

There rarely is a conflict between a person's strengths and the way that person performs. The two are complementary. But there is sometimes a conflict between a person's values and the same person's strengths. What one does well—even very well—and successfully may not fit with one's value system. It may not appear to that person as making a contribution and as something to which to devote one's life (or even a substantial portion thereof).

If I may inject a personal note: I too, many years ago, had to decide between what I was doing well and successfully, and my values. I was doing extremely well as a young investment banker in London in the mid-1930s; it clearly fitted my strengths. Yet I did not see myself making a contribution as an asset manager of any kind. People, I realized, were my values. And I saw no point in being the richest man in the cemetery. I had no money, no job in a deep Depression and no prospects. But I quit—and it was the right thing.

Values, in other words, are and should be the ultimate test.

II
Where Do I Belong?

The answers to the three questions: "What are my strengths? How do I perform? What are my values?" should enable the individual, and especially the individual knowledge worker, to decide where he or she belongs.

This is not a decision that most people can or should make at the beginning of their careers.

To be sure, a small minority know very early where they belong. Mathematicians, musicians or cooks, for instance, are usually mathematicians, musicians or cooks by the time they are four or five years old. Physicians usually decide in their teens, if not earlier. But most people, and especially highly gifted people, do not really know where they belong till they are well past their mid-twenties. By that time, however, they should know where their strengths are. They should know how they perform. And they should know what their values are.

And then they can and should decide where they belong. Or rather, they should be able to decide where they do *not belong*. The person who has learned that he or she does not really perform in a big organization should have learned to say "no" when offered a position in a big organization. The person who has learned that he or she is not a decision maker should have learned to say "no" when offered a decision-making assignment. A General Patton (who probably himself never learned it) should have learned to say "no" when offered an independent command, rather than a position as a high-level subordinate.

But also knowing the answer to these three questions enables people to say to an opportunity, to an offer, to an assignment: "Yes, I'll do that. But this is the way *I* should be doing it. This is the way it should be structured. This is the way my relationships should be. These are the kind of results you should expect from me, and in this time frame, because *this is who I am*."

Successful careers are not "planned." They are the careers of people who are prepared for the opportunity because they know their strengths, the way they work and their values. For knowing where one belongs makes ordinary people—hardworking, competent but mediocre otherwise—into outstanding performers.

III
What Is My Contribution?

To ask "What is my contribution?" means moving from knowledge to action. The question is not: "What do I *want* to contribute?" It is not: "What am I *told* to contribute?" It is: "What *should* I contribute?"

> This is a new question in human history. Traditionally, the task was given. It was given either by the work itself—as was the task of the peasant or the artisan. Or it was given by a master or a mistress, as was the task of the domestic servant. And, until very recently, it was taken for granted that most people were subordinates who did as they were told.

The advent of the knowledge worker is changing this, and fast. The first reaction to this change was to look at the employing *organization* to give the answer.

"Career Planning" is what the Personnel Department—especially of the large organization—was supposed to do in the 1950s and 1960s, for the "Organization Man," the new knowledge worker employee. In Japan it is still the way knowledge workers are being managed. But even in Japan the knowledge worker can increasingly expect to outlive the employing organization.

Except in Japan, however, the "Organization Man" and the career-planning Personnel Department have long become history. And with them disappeared the notion that anyone but oneself can—or should—be the "career planner." The reaction in the sixties was for knowledge people to ask: "What do I *want* to do?" People were told that "to do one's own thing" was the way to contribute. This was, for instance, what the "student rebellion" of 1968 believed.

We soon found out, however, that it was as wrong an answer as was the Organization Man. Very few of the people who believed that "doing one's own thing" leads to contribution, to self-fulfillment or to success achieved any of the three.

But still, there is no return to the old answer, that is, to do what you are being told, or what you are being assigned to. Knowledge workers, in particular, will have to learn to ask: "*What should MY contribution be?*" Only then should they ask: "Does this fit my strengths? Is this what I want to do?" And "Do I find this rewarding and stimulating?"

The best example I know of is the way Harry Truman repositioned himself when he became President of the United States, upon the sudden death of Franklin D. Roosevelt at the end of World War II. Truman had been picked for the Vice Presidency because he was totally concerned with domestic issues. For it was then generally believed that with the end of the war—and the end was clearly in sight— the U.S. would return to almost exclusive concern with domestic affairs. Truman had never shown the slightest interest in foreign affairs, knew nothing about them, and was kept in total ignorance of them. He was still totally focused on domestic affairs when, within a few weeks after his ascendancy, he went to the Potsdam Conference after Germany surrendered. There he sat for a week, with Churchill on one side and Stalin on the other, and realized, to his horror, that foreign affairs would dominate, but also that he knew absolutely nothing about them. He came back from Potsdam convinced that he had to give up what he wanted to do and instead had to concentrate on what he *had* to do, that is, on foreign affairs. He immediately—as already mentioned—put himself into school with General Marshall and Dean Acheson as his tutors. Within in a few months he was a master of foreign affairs and he, rather than Churchill or Stalin, created the postwar world—with his policy of containing Communism and pushing it back from Iran and Greece; with the Marshall Plan that rescued Western Europe; with the decision to rebuild Japan; and finally, with the call for worldwide economic development.

By contrast, Lyndon Johnson lost both the Vietnam War and his domestic policies because he clung to "What do I want to do?" instead of asking himself "What *should* my contribution be?"

Johnson, like Truman, had been entirely focused on domestic affairs. He too came into the Presidency wanting to complete what the New Deal had left unfinished. He very soon realized that the Vietnam War was what he *had* to concentrate on. But he could not give up what he *wanted* his contribution to be. He splintered himself between the Vietnam War and domestic reforms—and he lost both.

One more question has to be asked to decide "What should I contribute?": *"Where and how can I have results that make a difference?"*

The answer to this question has to balance a number of things. Results should be hard to achieve. They should require "stretching," to use the present buzzword. But they should be within reach. To aim at results that cannot be achieved—or can be achieved only under the most unlikely circumstances—is not being "ambitious." It is being foolish. At the same time, results should be meaningful. They should make a difference. And they should be visible and, if at all possible, measurable.

Here is one example from a nonprofit institution.

A newly appointed hospital administrator asked himself the question "What should be my contribution?" The hospital was big and highly prestigious. But it had been coasting on its reputation for thirty years and had become mediocre. The new hospital administrator decided that his contribution should be to establish a standard of excellence in one important area within two years. And so he decided to concentrate on turning around the Emergency Room and the Trauma Center—both big, visible and sloppy. The new hospital administrator thought through what to demand of an Emergency Room, and how to measure its performance. He decided that every patient who came into the Emergency Room had to be seen by a qualified nurse within sixty seconds. Within twelve months that hospital's Emergency Room had become a model for the entire United States. And its turnaround also showed that there can be standards, discipline, measurements in a hospital—and within another two years the whole hospital had been transformed.

The decision "What should my contribution be?" thus balances three elements. First comes the question: "What does the *situation* require?" Then comes the question: "How could *I* make the greatest *contribution* with my strengths, my way of performing, my values, to what needs to be done?" Finally, there is the question: "What *results* have to be achieved to make a difference?"

This then leads to the *action conclusions*: what to do, where to start, how to start, what goals and deadlines to set.

Throughout history, few people had any choices. The task was imposed on them either by nature or by a master. And so, in large measure, was the way in which they were supposed to perform the task. But so also were the expected results—they were given. To "do one's own thing" is, however, not freedom. It is license. It does not have results. It does not contribute. But to start out with the question *"What should I contribute?"* gives freedom. It gives freedom because it gives responsibility.

IV
Relationship Responsibility

Very few people work by themselves and achieve results by themselves—a few great artists, a few great scientists, a few great athletes. Most people work with other people and are effective through other people. That is true whether they are members of an organization or legally independent. To manage oneself, therefore, requires *taking relationship responsibility*.

There are two parts to it.

The first one is to accept the fact that other people are as much individuals as one is oneself. They insist on behaving like human beings. This means that they too have their strengths. It means that they too have their ways of getting things done. It means that they too have their values. To be effective, one therefore has to know the strengths, the performance modes and the values of the people one works with.

This sounds obvious. But few people pay attention to it.

Typical are people who, in their first assignment, worked for a man who is a reader. They therefore were trained in writing reports. Their next boss is a listener. But these people keep on writing reports to the new boss—the way President Johnson's assistants kept on writing reports to him because Jack Kennedy, who had hired them, had been a reader. Invariably, these people have no results. Invariably, their new boss thinks they are stupid, incompetent, lazy. They become failures. All that would have been needed to avoid this would have been *one* look at the boss and ask the question: "How does he or she perform?"

Bosses are not a title on the organization chart or a "function." They are individuals and entitled to do the work the way *they* do it. And it is incumbent on the people who work with them to observe them, to find out how they work and to adapt themselves to the way the bosses are effective.

There are bosses, for instance, who have to see the figures first—Alfred Sloan at General Motors was one of them. He himself was not a financial person but an engineer with strong marketing instincts. But as an engineer he had been trained to look first at figures.

Three of the ablest younger executives in General Motors did not make it into the top ranks because they did not look at Sloan—they did not realize that there was no point writing to him or talking to him until he first had spent time with the figures. They went in and presented their reports. Then they left the figures. But by that time they had lost Sloan.

As said before, readers are unlikely ever to become listeners, and listeners are unlikely ever to become readers. But everyone can learn to make a decent oral presentation or to write a decent report. It is simply the duty of the subordinate to enable the boss to do his or her work. And that requires looking at the boss and asking "What are his or her strengths? How does he or she do the work and perform? What are his or her values?" In fact, this is the secret of "managing" the boss.

One does the same with all the people one works with. Each of them works his or her way and not *my* way. And each of them is entitled to work in his or her way. What matters is whether they perform, and what their values are. How they perform—each is likely to do it differently. The first secret of effectiveness is to understand the people with whom one works and on whom one depends, and to make use of *their* strengths, *their* ways of working, *their* values. For working relations are as much based on the person as they are based on the work.

The second thing to do to manage oneself and to become effective is to *take responsibility for communications*. After people have thought through what their *strengths* are, how they *perform*, what their *values* are and especially what their *contribution* should be, they then have to ask: "Who needs to know this? On whom do I depend? And who depends on me?" And then one goes and tells all these people—and tells them in the way in which they receive a message, that is, in a memo if they are readers, or by talking to them if they are listeners and so on.

Whenever I—or any other consultant—have started to work with an organization, I am first told of all the "personality conflicts" within it. Most of them arise from the fact that one person does not know *what* the other person does, or does not know *how* the other person does his or her work, or does not know what *contribution* the other person concentrates on, and what results he or she expects. And the reason that they do not know is that they do not ask and therefore are not being told.

This reflects human stupidity less than it reflects human history. It was unnecessary until very recently to tell any of these things to anybody. Everybody in a district of the medieval city plied the same trade—there was a street of goldsmiths, and a street of shoemakers, and a street of armorers. (In Japan's Kyoto there are still the streets of the potters, the streets of the silk weavers, the streets of the lacquer makers.) One goldsmith knew exactly what every other goldsmith was doing; one shoemaker knew exactly what every other shoemaker was doing; one armorer knew exactly what every other armorer was doing. There was no need to explain anything. The same was true on the land where everybody in a valley planted the same crop as soon as the frost was out of the ground. There was no need to tell one's neighbor that one was going to plant potatoes—that, after all, was exactly what the neighbor did too, and at the same time.

And those few people who did things that were not "common," the few professionals, for instance, worked alone, and also did not have to tell anybody what they were doing. Today the great majority of people work with others who do different things.

As said before, the marketing vice-president may have come out of sales and knows everything about sales. But she knows nothing about promotion and pricing and advertising and packaging and sales planning, and so on— she has never done any of these things. Then it is incumbent on the people who do these things to make sure that the marketing vice-president understands what they are trying to do, why they are trying to do it, how they are going to do it and what results to expect.

If the marketing vice-president does not understand what these high-grade knowledge specialists are doing, it is primarily *their* fault, and not that of the marketing vice-president. They have not told her. They have not educated her. Conversely, it is the marketing vice-president's responsibility to make sure that every one of the people she works with understands how *she* looks on marketing, what her goals are, how she works and what she expects of herself and of every one of them.

Even people who understand the importance of relationship responsibility often do not tell their associates and do not ask them. They are afraid of being thought presumptuous, inquisitive or stupid. *They are wrong.* Whenever anyone goes to his or her associates and says: "This is *what* I am good at. This is *how* I work. These are my *values.* This is the contribution I plan to concentrate on and the results I should be expected to deliver," the response is *always*: "This is *most helpful.* But why haven't you told me *earlier*?"

And one gets the same reaction—without a single exception in my experience—if one then asks: "And what do I need to know about *your* strengths, how *you* perform, your *values* and your proposed *contribution*?"

In fact, a knowledge worker should request of people with whom he or she works—whether as subordinates, superiors, colleagues, team members—that they adjust their behavior to the knowledge worker's strengths, and to the way the knowledge worker works. Readers should request that their associates *write* to them, listeners should request that their associates first *talk* to them and so on. And again, whenever that is being done, the reaction of the other person will be: "Thanks for telling me. It's enormously helpful. But why didn't you ask me earlier?"

Organizations are no longer built on force. They are increasingly built on trust. Trust does not mean that people like one another. It means that people can trust one another. And this presupposes that people understand one another. Taking relationship responsibility is therefore an absolute necessity. *It is a duty.* Whether one is a member of the organization, a consultant to it, a supplier to it, a distributor, one owes relationship responsibility to every one with whom one works, on whose work one depends; and who in turn depends on one's own work.

V
The Second Half of Your Life

As said before: For the first time in human history, individuals can expect to outlive organizations. This creates a totally new challenge: *What to do with the second half of one's life?*

One can no longer expect that the organization for which one works at age thirty will still be around when one reaches age sixty. But also, forty or fifty years in the same kind of work is much too long for most people. They deteriorate, get bored, lose all joy in their work, "retire on the job" and become a burden to themselves and to everyone around them.

This is not necessarily true of the very top achievers such as very great artists. Claude Monet (1840–1926), the greatest Impressionist painter, was still painting masterpieces in his eighties, and working twelve hours a day, even though he had lost almost all his eyesight. Pablo Picasso (1881–1973), perhaps the greatest Post-Impressionist painter, similarly painted till he died in his nineties—and in his seventies invented a new style. The greatest musical instrumentalist of this century, the Spanish cellist Pablo Casals (1876–1973), planned to perform a new piece of music and practiced it on the very day on which he died at age ninety-seven. But these are the rarest of exceptions even among very great achievers. Neither Max Planck (1858–1947) nor Albert Einstein (1879–1955), the two giants of modern physics, did important scientific work after their forties. Planck had *two* more careers. After 1918—aged sixty—he reorganized German science. After being forced into retirement by the Nazis in 1933, he, in

1945, almost ninety, started once more to rebuild German science after Hitler's fall. But Einstein retired in his forties to become a "famous man."

There is a great deal of talk today about the "mid-life crisis" of the executive. It is mostly boredom. At age forty-five most executives have reached the peak of their business career and know it. After twenty years of doing very much the same kind of work, they are good at their jobs. But few are learning anything anymore, few are contributing anything anymore and few expect the job again to become a challenge and a satisfaction.

Manual workers who have been working for forty years—in the steel mill for instance, or in the cab of a locomotive—are physically and mentally tired long before they reach the end of their normal life expectancy, that is, well before they reach even traditional retirement age. They are "finished." If they survive—and their life expectancy too has gone up to an average of seventy-five years or so—they are quite happy spending ten or fifteen years doing nothing, playing golf, going fishing, engaging in some minor hobby and so on. But knowledge workers are not "finished." They are perfectly capable of functioning despite all kinds of minor complaints. And yet the original work that was so challenging when the knowledge worker was thirty has become a deadly bore when the knowledge worker is fifty—and still he or she is likely to face another fifteen if not another twenty years of work.

To manage oneself, therefore, will increasingly require preparing oneself for the second half of one's life. (The best books on this subject are by Bob Buford—a very successful businessman who himself has created his own second half of life. They are *Half Time* [Grand Rapids: Zondervan, 1994] and *Game Plan* [Grand Rapids: Zondervan, 1997].)

There are three answers:
The first is actually to start a second and different career (as Max Planck did). Often this means only moving from one kind of an organization to another.

Typical are the middle-level American business executives who in substantial numbers move to a hospital, a university or some other nonprofit organization, around age forty-five or forty-eight, when the children are grown and the retirement pension is vested. In many cases they stay in the same kind of work. The divisional controller in the big corporation becomes, for instance, controller in a medium-sized hospital. But there are also a growing number of people who actually move into a different line of work. Increasingly, for instance, students in American Protestant theological seminaries are forty-five—rather than twenty-five—years old. They made a first career in business or government—some in medicine—and then, when the children are grown, move into the ministry. And so did a friend of mine who, after thirty years as a successful art museum director and curator, entered a seminary at age 55.

In the United States there is a fairly substantial number of middle-aged women who have worked for twenty years, in business or in local government, have risen to a junior management position and now, at age forty-five and with the children grown, enter law school. Three or four years later they then establish themselves as small-time lawyers in their local communities.

We will see much more of such second-career people who have achieved fair success in their first job. These people have substantial skills, for example, the divisional controller who moves into the local community hospital. They know how to work. They need a community—and the house is empty with the children gone. They need the income, too. But above all, they need the challenge.

The Parallel Career

The second answer to the question of what to do with the second half of one's life is to develop a *parallel* career.

A large and rapidly growing number of people—especially

people who are very successful in their first careers—stay in the work they have been doing for twenty or twenty-five years. Many keep on working forty or fifty hours a week in their main and paid job. Some move from busy full-time to being part-time employees or become consultants. But then they create for themselves a parallel job—usually in a nonprofit organization—and one that often takes another ten hours of work a week. They take over the administration of their church, for instance, or the presidency of the local Girl Scouts Council, they run the battered women shelter, they work for the local public library as children's librarian, they sit on the local school board and so on.

And then, finally, the third answer—there are the "social entrepreneurs." These are usually people who have been very successful in their first profession, as businessmen, as physicians, as consultants, as university professors. They love their work, but it no longer challenges them. In many cases they keep on doing what they have been doing all along, though they spend less and less of their time on it. But they *start* another, and usually a nonprofit, activity.

Here are some examples—beginning with Bob Buford, the author of the two books, mentioned above, about preparing for the second half of one's life. Having built a very successful television and radio business, Buford still keeps on running it. But he first started and built a successful nonprofit organization to make the Protestant churches in America capable of survival; now he is building a second, equally successful organization to teach other social entrepreneurs how to manage their own private, nonprofit ventures while still running their original businesses. But there is also the equally successful lawyer—legal counsel to a big corporation—who has started a venture to establish model schools in his state.

People who manage the "second half" may always be a minority only. The majority may keep doing what they are doing now, that is, to retire on the job, being bored, keeping on with their routine and counting the years until retirement. But it will be this minority, the people who see the long working-life expectancy as an opportunity both for themselves and for society, who may increasingly become the leaders and the models. They, increasingly, will be the "success stories."

There is one requirement for managing the second half of one's life: to begin creating it long before one enters it.

When it first became clear thirty years ago that working-life expectancies were lengthening very fast, many observers (including myself) believed that retired people would increasingly become volunteers for American nonprofit institutions. This has not happened. If one does not begin to volunteer before one is forty or so, one will not volunteer when past sixty.

Similarly, all the social entrepreneurs I know began to work in their chosen second enterprise long before they reached their peak in their original business. The lawyer mentioned above began to do volunteer legal work for the schools in his state when he was around thirty-five. He got himself elected to a school board at age forty. When he reached fifty, and had amassed a substantial fortune, he then started his own enterprise to build and run model schools. He is, however, still working near-full-time as the lead counsel in the very big company that, as a very young lawyer, he had helped found.

There is another reason that managing yourself will increasingly mean that the knowledge worker develops a second *major interest*, and develops it early.

No one can expect to live very long without experiencing a serious setback in one's life or in one's work.

There is the competent engineer who at age forty-two is being passed over for promotion in the company. There is the competent college professor who at age forty-two realizes that she will stay forever in the small college in which she got her first appointment and will never get the professorship at the big university—even though she may be fully qualified for it. There are tragedies in one's personal family life—the breakup of one's marriage, the loss of a child.

And then a second major interest—and not just another hobby—may make all the difference. The competent engineer passed over for promotion now knows that he has not been very successful in his job. But in his outside activity—for example, as treasurer in his local church—he has achieved success and continues to have success. One's own family may break up, but in that outside activity there is still a community.

This will be increasingly important in a society in which *success* has become important.

Historically there was no such thing. The overwhelming majority of people did not expect anything but to stay in their "proper station," as an old English prayer has it. The only mobility there was downward mobility. Success was practically unknown.

In a knowledge society we expect everyone to be a "success." But this is clearly an impossibility. For a great many people there is, at best, absence of failure. For where there is success, there has to be failure. And then it is vitally important for the individual—but equally for the individual's family—that there be an area in which the individual contributes, makes a difference, and is *somebody*. That means having a second area, whether a second career, a parallel career, a social venture, a serious outside interest, all of them offering an opportunity for being a leader, for being respected, for being a success.

The changes and challenges of Managing Oneself may seem obvious, if not elementary, compared to the changes and challenges discussed in the earlier chapters. And the answers may seem to be self-evident to the point of appearing naïve. To be sure, many topics in the earlier chapters—for example, Being a Change

Leader or some of the Information Challenges—are far more complex and require more advanced and more difficult policies, technologies, methodologies. But most of the new behavior—the new policies, technologies, methodologies—called for in these earlier chapters can be considered EVOLUTIONS.

Managing Oneself is a REVOLUTION in human affairs. It requires new and unprecedented things from the individual, and especially from the knowledge worker. For in effect it demands that each knowledge worker *think* and behave as a *Chief Executive Officer*. It also requires an almost 180-degree change in the knowledge workers' thoughts and actions from what most of us—even of the younger generation—still take for granted as the way to think and the way to act. Knowledge workers, after all, first came into being in any substantial numbers a generation ago. (I coined the term "knowledge worker," but only thirty years ago, in my 1969 book *The Age of Discontinuity*.)

But also the shift from manual workers who do as they are being told—either by the task or by the boss—to knowledge workers who have to manage themselves profoundly challenges social structure. For every existing society, even the most "individualist" one, takes two things for granted, if only subconsciously: Organizations outlive workers, and most people stay put. Managing Oneself is based on the very opposite *realities*: Workers are likely to outlive organizations, and the knowledge worker has mobility.

In the United States MOBILITY is accepted. But even in the United States, workers outliving organizations—and with it the need to be prepared for a *Second and Different Half of One's Life*—is a revolution for which practically no one is prepared. Nor is any existing institution, for example, the present retirement system. In the rest of the developed world, however, *immobility* is expected and accepted. It is "stability."

> In Germany, for instance, mobility—until very recently—came to an end with the individual's reaching age ten or, at the latest, age sixteen. If a child did not enter *Gymnasium* at age ten, he or she had lost any chance ever to go to the university. And the apprenticeship that the great majority who did not go to the *Gymnasium* entered

at age fifteen or sixteen as a mechanic, a bank clerk, a cook—irrevocably and irreversibly—decided what work the person was going to do the rest of his or her life. Moving from the occupation of one's apprenticeship into another occupation was simply not done even when not actually forbidden.

The developed society that faces the greatest challenge and will have to make the most difficult changes is the society that has been most successful in the last fifty years: Japan. Japan's success—and there is no precedent for it in history—very largely rested on *organized immobility*—the immobility of "lifetime employment." In lifetime employment it is the organization that manages the individual. And it does so, of course, on the assumption that the individual has no choice. The individual is being managed.

I very much hope that Japan will find a solution that *preserves* the social stability, the community—and the social harmony—that lifetime employment provided, and yet creates the mobility that knowledge work and knowledge workers must have. Far more is at stake than Japan's own society and civic harmony. A Japanese solution would provide a model—for in every country a functioning society does require cohesion. Still, a successful Japan will be a very different Japan.

But so will be every other developed country. The emergence of the knowledge worker who both *can* and *must* manage himself or herself is transforming every society.

This book has intentionally confined itself to MANAGE-MENT CHALLENGES. Even in this last chapter, it has talked about the individual, that is, the knowledge worker. But the changes discussed in this book go way beyond management. They go way beyond the individual and his or her career. What this book actually dealt with is:

THE FUTURE OF SOCIETY.

Acknowledgments

This book grew out of a suggestion by my long-time American editor, Cass Canfield, Jr., of HarperCollins. It is, however, a very different book from the one Mr. Canfield and I originally envisaged. We thought of a book that would bring together in one volume the best from the management books I have written and published for more than fifty years—a kind of "Drucker Retrospective." But as I began to work on the book Mr. Canfield suggested, it became increasingly clear to both of us that what was appropriate was not a book looking backward. It was one that looks AHEAD. As a result, this book contains NOTHING that is an excerpt from earlier management books of mine. It *supplements* them by LOOKING AHEAD. And all the time, while working on this book, I have had—as I have had for many, many years—the benefit of Mr. Canfield's advice, suggestions, comments—they have greatly improved this book.

But this book also celebrates SIXTY years of close association with my UK publisher, Butterworth/Heinemann. Since the firm—then Wm. Heinemann—published my first book, *The End of Economic Man*, in 1939, I have had no other publisher in the UK and in the countries of the Commonwealth. It is an association I greatly treasure. I am delighted that this book of mine will again appear under the Heinemann imprint.

As readers see in Chapter Three, I preach *piloting the new*, that is, testing it on a small scale. And, for once, I practice what I preach. I pilot-test a new book. One way is to distribute early drafts and copies to a few friends—mostly longtime clients—and ask for their candid reaction. Again and again I have changed something, rewritten a section, clarified an issue, as a result of their comments and criticism. But the best pilot-test for my writings, I have found, is to prepublish sections of a forthcoming book in magazines. This does TWO things. I get reactions from readers—and they tell me both what might need changing and where I need to explain or clarify. I owe a great debt to the people—mostly strangers—who write in, comment on or criticize one of these prepublished pieces, and especially to those who—often loudly—dissent. My thanks to them all. But, above all, prepublishing in a magazine gives me the inestimable benefit of being EDITED. I cannot even begin to do justice to what I owe the editors of these magazines—for their questions, their guidance, their cutting, rephrasing, repositioning. Especially thanks are due to Jim Michaels and Rich Karlgaard of *Forbes* magazine (which prepublished sections of Chapter One and the first part of Chapter Four), to Gunders Strads of the *California Management Review* (which prepublished an abridged version of Chapter Five), and to Nan Stone of the *Harvard Business Review* (which prepublished sections of Chapter Four and Chapter Six). They greatly helped to make this a better book.

Index

BOOKS BY PETER F. DRUCKER

THE DAILY DRUCKER

**366 Days of Insight and Motivation
for Getting the Right Things Done**

ISBN 0-06-074244-5 (hardcover)
366 daily readings harvested from Drucker's
lifetime of work by Jospeh A. Maciariello.

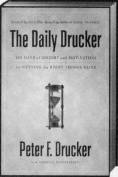

THE ESSENTIAL DRUCKER

**The Best of Sixty Years
of Peter Drucker's Essential Writings
on Management**

ISBN 0-06-621087-9 (hardcover)
ISBN 0-06-093574-X (paperback)
Covers the basic principles and concerns of management
and its problems, challenges, and opportunities.

THE EFFECTIVE EXECUTIVE

ISBN 0-06-051607-0 (paperback)
Demonstrates the distinctive skill of the
executive and offers fresh insights into old and
seemingly obvious business situations.

MANAGING THE NON-PROFIT ORGANIZATION

Principles and Practices

ISBN 0-887-30601-2 (paperback)
Gives examples and explanations of mission,
leadership, resources, marketing, goals, people
development, decision making, and much more.

INNOVATION AND ENTREPRENEURSHIP

ISBN 0-887-30618-7 (paperback)
A superbly practical book that explains what established businesses, public survey institutions, and new ventures have to know, have to learn, and have to do in today's economy and marketplace.

THE PRACTICE OF MANAGEMENT

ISBN 0-887-30613-6 (paperback)
ISBN 1-559-94278-9 (audio)
The first book to depict management as a distinct function and to recognize managing as a separate responsibility, this classic work by Peter F. Drucker is the fundamental and basic book for understanding these ideas.

MANAGEMENT
Tasks, Responsibilities, Practices

ISBN 0-887-30615-2 (paperback)
Equips the manager with the understanding, the thinking, the knowledge, and the skills for today's and also tomorrow's jobs.

MANAGING FOR RESULTS

ISBN 0-887-30614-4 (paperback)
Combines specific economic analysis with a grasp of the entrepreneurial force in business prosperity.

All titles are also available as ebooks from PerfectBound